NEVER A DULL MOMENT

The sequel to the bestselling and critically acclaimed

"Wellies and Warders"

By

Dave Ginnelly

Copyright © Dave Ginnelly 2016
This book is sold subject to the condition that it shall not, by way of trade or otherwise, be lent, resold, hired out, or otherwise circulated without the publisher's prior consent in any form of binding or cover other than that in which it is published and without a similar condition including this condition being imposed on the subsequent publisher.
The moral right of Dave Ginnelly has been asserted.
ISBN-13: 978-1530944774
ISBN-10: 1530944775

DEDICATION

This book is dedicated to
DOORWAY
Dugdale Street
Nuneaton

CONTENTS

Chapter 1 .... *1*
Chapter 2 .... *10*
Chapter 3 .... *18*
Chapter 4 .... *27*
Chapter 5 .... *34*
Chapter 6 .... *43*
Chapter 7 .... *51*
Chapter 8 .... *60*
Chapter 9 .... *69*
Chapter 10 .... *76*
Chapter 11 .... *85*
Chapter 12 .... *93*
Chapter 13 .... *102*
Chapter 14 .... *109*
Chapter 15 .... *117*
Chapter 16 .... *125*
Chapter 17 .... *133*
Chapter 18 .... *141*
Chapter 19 .... *148*
Chapter 20 .... *154*
Chapter 21 .... *162*
Chapter 22 .... *171*
Chapter 23 .... *179*
Chapter 24 .... *186*
Chapter 25 .... *194*
Chapter 26 .... *203*
Chapter 27 .... *212*
Chapter 28 .... *221*

ACKNOWLEDGMENTS

I would like to acknowledge that none of this book would have even be put to paper without the encouragement and support of the following people.

Jason Ashby

Lisa Ashby

Dale Barnwell

Debbie Knights

Andy Crampton

Neil Salter

*

R I P Andy Crampton 1957 to 2016

The time you had left was precious my good friend and I feel honoured that even though you knew you still chose to complete my book... I could never thank you enough... gone but never forgotten.

You were unique. Sadly missed.

CHAPTER 1

So how do we define a "criminal" and who actually reaches that conclusion?

My name is David Brian Ginnelly and I was born on December 9th 1953 in Dewsbury, West Yorkshire. I've been led to believe my middle name was in association with my mother's favourite film star, a man called David Brian who apparently was a famous film star of the time. Not that I have ever come across any of his films, so it's either a debatable or dubious title, is the word "famous".

I grew up to be a criminal who spent many years in penal establishments, but how did that come about? Textbook experts will have us believe it's all in the genes, but I would doubt that very much as I doubt my father or his father before him had even set foot in a courtroom, let alone spent time under lock and key.

Circumstances dictate what many of us are to become and I was born into a period of time when the consumer society was just beginning to evolve, and the introduction of television sets and other *"must have"* consumer goods were readily available should the general public have the means at their disposal.

The very beginning of *"keeping up with the Smiths and Joneses"* of the period, and don't get me wrong, nothing stands in the way of progress and that will always be the way of the society in which we live.

I, along with many others, would not have set out to become a criminal but unfortunately I would steal at almost every opportunity, as I will explain in later chapters, and my fate seemed sealed; this was how my life was to pan out.

Even to this day, when it seems to be that my life has taken a turn for the better, I would in no way describe myself as *"rehabilitated"* or *"reformed"* because I am still criminal-minded, because it has been a way of life. Some people live their lives in a saint-like and orderly manner and others, such as myself, prefer being on the edge of society. Once you find yourself in a prison on regular occasions it never then, or could now, hold any fears for me.

I have sometimes been fortunate enough to stay out of the penal system for over a decade, but even after such a period of time there is little to be concerned about because the whole scenario is the exact same as in previous decades, and this is despite the introduction of the Home Office Inspectors of Prisons making regular visits and inspections. Little or no rehabilitation comes from being detained in a prison.

A number of things can contribute to individuals taking that wrong turn and it's all well and good "hard liners" coming out of the woodwork to suggest the re-introduction of corporal punishment, but nobody had more of that than me and I can safely say it served no purpose with the few of us that seemed to constantly be on the mat, returning for more of the same on numerous occasions.

Schooling was harsh and it seemed that to be one of the nuns required to perform their role, they had to be between four and five feet tall and very stern-faced, with not an ounce of compassion. On reflection it's obvious that these ladies would not have experienced much romance in their formative years, and I doubt very much there would have been any likelihood of them finding it in later years.

In the world of fantasy and film making, nuns are regularly portrayed as beautiful young women who have chosen a vow of silence for whatever reason, but let me assure you that the sisters who led prayers at my school, St Paulinus Dewsbury in West Yorkshire, would have turned anyone into stone like Medusa as their faces were that frightening. It is funny, looking back, because all of them were of a similar height to the children they were trying to teach. Maybe their mission was to give the children direction and discipline in life but I am sure that anyone attending any Catholic school in later years will not have fond memories. Everything is to do with religion. I would grasp this as quickly as I could because it could save me quite often from either getting the cane or ruler or both on my hands.

The stations of the cross. The ashes on my

forehead. The rosary bead prayers. I would gather the information quickly like a sponge does with water. I knew everything, whereas nowadays I could tell you little or nothing about my religion as I lost my faith many, many years ago.

We would be called upon to bring money in each day to donate to some charity or other, and the nuns would create a competitive feel about proceedings by announcing that the one who brought the most money in by the end of the week would be given some tiny photograph, about the size of a matchbox, of Sister Benedictine or Sister Bernadette or some other latter-day saint and certainly not something, in my opinion, worthy of treasuring.

All of the other kids would be rushing to school each morning clutching whatever pennies or three penny bits that they had managed to obtain, and ours was on an estate in which we lacked pocket money because the nuns seemed to squeeze every last penny out of the different classrooms. Of course I had every sympathy with the photos of whatever starving African children (the cause of the day at the time) they would show us, but if they had taken the time out to check the waistline of yours truly they would have discovered that I did not get a meal myself some days at home, because we ourselves were poor.

Needless to say I would not make the effort and would prefer spending my pennies on catapults or pea shooters or other disruptive toys that small boys preferred at the time. Of course I had the devil in me and no amount of holy water could have saved my soul, and most certainly not some photograph of the bleeding heart of Saint Agnes or whoever.

So obviously I did not enter into the spirit of things and used to get a ruler across the back of my hands or fingers quite often, and the rulers these sisters of virtue carried upon them in no way resembled the wafer-thin rulers which we have today. These rulers were the width of a cricket bat, or seemed that way at the time through the eyes of a child.

On one particular occasion when the whole day consisted of me being given the ruler on the hand in the classroom or caned in the headmistress's study (yet another four-foot ogre), and my hand being very bruised and tender, I awoke to discover that I had a floppy index finger and upon further investigation at the local hospital it was found I needed a splint to keep a broken finger in place. I had the bonus of being unable to do any schoolwork in the classroom and I just spent the day staring out of the window and daydreaming.

God knows what health and safety would make of such incidents nowadays, but then it was quite the "norm" and to expect any sympathy at home would be a lost cause because my father and grandmother would simply believe that I had caused my own injury whilst playing football after school had finished. Nobody would ever dare question the actions of the nuns.

This was a very strong Catholic community and discipline at school or at home was always part of the agenda and just accepted without challenge. It was quite a funny period in my life because my grandmother was quite a small lady and I just seemed to be continually surrounded by small females, all a bit of a surreal environment. It was around this time that I lost interest in school and I suppose that I could not wait for the final bell of the day to ring.

I would never be in a rush to get home and I would either wile away the hours at the local library and eventually the pet shop, where I was absolutely amazed by the array of pets and in particular a monkey that I was allowed to feed peanuts and formed a bond with. I begged and begged for this to be my Christmas present and obviously I appreciate now that the granting of my wish was simply to gain a little peace and quiet in the home.

I had told everyone in and out of school that I was getting a monkey for Christmas and for them to come down on Christmas morning, only to be told that it was a foolish and impossible idea. This devastated me and I was left open to ridicule from my school friends and I dreaded returning to school after the Christmas break.

Instead of the monkey I was given a very small transistor radio and a bag of fruit which I subsequently threw up the wall. I was inconsolable as I ran out of the family home in the direction of the pet shop to look through the window, only to find that my soulmate was not there in its usual place and the shop was closed for Christmas Day. *Bastards, the lot of you*, I thought, *and no way will I be in attendance at your church with all of your pious, sanctimonious faces and supposedly happy families pretence.*

This was to be my first lesson of disappointment and broken promises in life, and once the shop opened again and I discovered the monkey no longer resided there, I also came to the conclusion the proprietor was a part of the whole conspiracy and he had in fact sold the monkey to another small boy. It was these thoughts that perhaps led me to commit my first ever acts of stealing things that did not belong to me.

I was always a poor child and could often be seen wearing a pair of wellington boots. I proceeded to put two small birds in one boot and a mouse in the other. I would never draw suspicion because I would often be in attendance at the shop without purchasing anything, and perhaps the owner felt a little sorry for me and gave me the run of the mill. I left the shop and released the birds which I now know was a cruel thing to do, but I felt I owed the owner a little payback.

My rewards due to the theft meant little or nothing if I'm honest, but the excitement that went with the adrenalin of that first theft was to remain with me. I liked it! I was hooked and that feeling would remain with me for many years. I had just committed my first criminal offence – theft – and I had enjoyed it and there would be no turning back.

I played with my mouse for the rest of the day, always careful to conceal it out of fear that I may be asked how I had obtained it. I would feel it run around inside my wellington boot and was very comforted by its presence. It would occasionally go to school with me and I hated one nun in particular for always teasing me and asking me how my monkey was coming on, but I used to ignore her as best I could and think to myself, *Sod you, I have now stolen and gone against all you have tried to instil in me.*

I hated school and I hated home and I think it had all started to go wrong even at that early age, but I would not appreciate just how much until later years and my constant run-ins with the local constabulary.

My criminal behaviour could not and should not be determined by genetics, but I am almost sure that broken promises, brutal nuns, and obsessive religious preaching played a key part. When a child is a child then let them be so, instead of scaring them with religion before they even draw breath. For Christ's sake, even on our first communion you had us all in fear that should the communion touch our teeth it was a mortal sin, or an original sin, or whatever sin was the flavour of the day.

I didn't enjoy any of the religion at all but I had enjoyed breaking one of its commandments by stealing, and I would very shortly be a fully-fledged criminal. I was about to become a fallen angel and I could not wait – just how bad, you will discover in later chapters. But meanwhile, I had one last act of divine retribution to contend with.

Obviously I could not conceal the mouse at all times of the day and on one of the occasions I had to secrete my purloined pet. I made the rash decision of placing the mouse at the back of the tins of food in the pantry, but the realisation that this was a major error soon came to light with the continued loud screams of my grandmother from the kitchen.

Close to the kitchen was an enclosed area on the landing where the dustbins were kept and a house brick wedged against the door to prevent it from constantly opening. By the time I reached the kitchen from the upper floor, the deed had already been done and the mouse was no more, and I could see traces of blood on the corner of the brick.

It mattered little because I already knew I could steal another at any time should I choose to, and so the divine warning from above would go unheeded as I progressed to thefts of a more rewarding nature.

My grandmother had sealed the mouse's fate but I had by now, sealed my own fate also.

CHAPTER 2

Dewsbury Celtic Working Men's Club was the meeting place of all of the local community and also comprised all of the local sports teams, as long as they were sporting the "green and white" hoops with allegiance to everything Catholic.

We, as children, would be encouraged to be in attendance at these events with the hope that many would become the next generation of players for the teams, but I was built like a matchstick and had no inclination to be trying to tackle someone to the ground who was twice the size of myself, and God forbid anyone should ever pass the ball to me or I wouldn't have stopped running until I reached the next county.

Most local games would be played in Dewsbury Crow's Nest Park and all of the children would gather round, and when half time approached, would stand around in the hope of getting one of the small segments of orange provided for the players. More fool them as I had richer pickings on my mind, as I doubled back to the dressing rooms that were situated below the clubhouse. They would never be locked and to not arouse suspicion I would quickly race around and take a little silver out of each pocket where I could hear the sound of coins making contact with other coins. I had no need to take an overly great amount because my needs were little at that age. Not once in perhaps a two-year period of doing this did I get caught, and I even had the nerve to get on the team bus for away games with the free transport provided.

Perhaps it never came to light because I wouldn't steal expensive jewellery and the small amounts of change would go unnoticed. I would have no fear of repeating the self-same routine in away dressing rooms because I had the ready-made excuse that my father had sent me to get his cigarettes, an excuse that I never needed to use.

It is perhaps worth noting that this was a hard drinking community and many of these rugby players would be half cut with alcohol before they even took to the pitch, and mislaid money would easily be overlooked. I would often be strolling about with lots of change in my pockets and at such an early age, realising this could be done this easily, just set my life in stone. I would never leave any shop without placing something in my pocket. Stealing had become a big part of my life and even though I had pockets of money I would still rather not pay for things. Even at that early age it was far too late to change. The simple fact being, I could not have done so even if I had wanted to.

I was hooked on the excitement and craved bigger and better exploits.

I had noticed in a local shop ran by a Mrs Clark, that once a customer left her shop, the front door would take an eternity to close once she had returned to her living room to watch television. The only time she would need to resurface would be when she heard the bell chime when another customer entered the shop, but I had already placed my foot against the door to prevent it closing and very quickly placed something weighty there, giving me time to race to and sit on the counter and grab myself as many packs of cigarettes as I could carry.

I would let the door inch slowly shut once I had got my ill-gotten gains and no one was any the wiser, and I was able to do this again and again for months to come.

I did do what the other children on the estate did and played football or cricket for long periods as well, but I had become a thief, and when the opportunity came about, I took it. It's difficult to explain why I did these things, they just seemed to take over. Nobody seemed to have much of anything and even motor cars seemed to be a rarity in those days.

We would set up a cricket game in the middle of the street with perhaps five house bricks propping up a piece of wooden boarding and maybe once an hour a car would come by and we would need to stand at the side of the road with the bricks until it passed, then resume the game, and this was a main thoroughfare.

We had lots of fun times as kids but I would only play cricket if the ball was an old "spongy" type, one where if it hit you it would not bruise you, whereas if it was a proper cricket ball I would give that game a miss due to previous hospital visits. The older boys would bowl it at you with some force, with the intention of hitting you rather than the wicket. I was more than a little accident prone and could be seen regularly at the outpatients' of the local hospital.

I was a latter-day Mr Magoo and always in some accident or other, even to the extent that I used to get invited to the hospital Christmas party each year. Either because of my accidents or perhaps my shabby appearance, who knows, but I was invited on two consecutive occasions.

I would relish the pleasure of those play periods but I would always be wary of telling any of the other kids what I had been up to, and in particular the older boys who would have just taken my money and cigarettes from me. It was a crazy childhood but at least when summer was summer it was exactly that, and six weeks off school represented continual sunshine of the hottest kind and the seasons went with the flow. The only reason we would ever need coats or pullovers would be as a makeshift goalpost to play football.

The estate that I grew up in, Westtown, was a beautiful place to grow up, for all that poverty was rife in the area. The actual flats have long gone and have been replaced by one of the UK's biggest mosques, and I feel in a way my childhood place of birth has been stolen.

I was living in the flats on High Street when some of the first immigrants arrived in the country, if I remember correctly, Indians and Pakistanis. If my memory serves, the one who moved in underneath our flat was called Mr Hookemdad and of course I had been given the parental warnings about not causing trouble and making everyone welcome, but that was like a red rag to a bull with me and I spent a good half an hour one day lowering a tea spoon tied to a string, and swinging it outwards until it tapped on the window.

Mr Hookemdad would occasionally open his window to attempt to grab the spoon but I would reel it up much faster than he anticipated, until finally he managed to grab it, but not before I had warmed the spoon up on the gas ring in the kitchen. He screamed obscenities in his own native tongue and I ran to bolt the door before he came up the other flights of steps to pound on our door. I was safely locked away and out of harm's way, but later that evening when my father finished work a fist fight ensued in the yard between the pair of them, which culminated in me also taking a couple of blows from my father.

But who cared? We had just had a fun-packed day filled with laughter, but I avoided Mr Hookemdad for months after that incident.

The next immigrant resident, a Mr Shah, actually moved in next door and was always to be seen in his uniform as he worked for the local bus company. My grandmother thought that Mr Shah was a perfect gentleman and told me not to dare antagonise him, and so when he gave me a note one day and a couple of shillings to run an errand for him, I readily agreed.

I was to go to a local area which was hugely populated by immigrants, and it was a very strange sort of corner shop with lots of men stood about shaking hands and making lots of conversation. A glass display cabinet had lots of strange-coloured curly sweet stuff in it, which I was offered, but refused as they differed greatly from English delicacies. The man whom I had given the note to had vanished out the back of the shop and came back in holding a chicken by its legs, which I thought nothing about until he brought a big machete down and – WHOOSH – in one chop took the bird's head clean off.

Jesus Christ, what just happened? I stood there, frozen to the spot in shock, and could not believe what I had just witnessed. I was as white as a sheet when he passed the bird to me, now wrapped in newspaper and very warm still. I tucked it under my arm and I walked home in shock, and don't think I spoke another word to anyone for the rest of the day.

I'm really sorry Mr Shah, but bollocks to community relations. I will be requiring a sight more than two shillings to be ever running that errand again.

It confused me for weeks how the bird had continued to live for a while even without its head. *Sod that.* I thought, *let's get back to sending the hot spoon down below.* Not really, I wouldn't have dared.

I began to experiment with lots of things about now, beginning with my grandmother's medication.

I'd heard her say to one of the neighbours how her new medication from the doctor had made her all "fuzzy" and dizzy, and I thought, *I will have a sample of that*. My second opinion is that she was very much right as I continued to be a little "fuzzy" and dizzy for the next week or so as I sampled more and more. Next, I used to enjoy the feeling of gas after I had left the dentist and decided it couldn't be any worse, and so I fed the gas pipe in our kitchen into a pint of milk until it bubbled and then I drank it.

Well what can I say? It was certainly a different experience but certainly not to be recommended to everyone, although having said that, the gas of today is totally different. It just seemed as though I needed devilment every single day and I didn't care who I upset.

I was not the only one misbehaving though, as I used to witness a married man visiting one of the other female neighbours, and although I wouldn't know for sure what was actually taking place, it seemed it was very untoward. I threw a few stones at the door and when the man popped his head out I pelted him with a few water balloons but his anger surprised me as he chased me. Oh no. This chase went on for mile after mile and I'd almost run into a dead end when I noticed that St Paulinus Church was open and foolishly believing he would not come in there after me, I ran inside, but I was his prey and enter the church he did.

Not once had I ever been within a mile of the choir or what it entailed but I either remained where I was at the altar and became a sacrificial slaughter, or sprinted down that vestry like a greyhound out of its trap. I was down those stairs like the wind, saying a quick prayer as I went.

After this episode I made a conscious decision to

stop antagonising the neighbours.

I believe my pursuer in this case was Polish, although he ran like an Ethiopian or Kenyan and my days were numbered with some of them.

I was misunderstood in my opinions; I simply had a sense of adventure and I would certainly need that attribute for what the rest of my life was about to put me through.

I had slowly morphed into a criminal of sorts but I don't think that necessarily made me a bad person. Maybe I was rebelling against all that the Catholic Church represented.

I'm sorry to anyone who feels different but to me it was soul destroying and my faith is very much weaker now I am older. Any present-day confessional box, I would need to be in there perhaps for six months to gain absolution, and yet despite this I still have high morals and standards better than most supposed Christians.

CHAPTER 3

I still did many things that all small children did and we had our own little gang, and most days we would do death-defying stunts that would give all of the parents sleepless nights wondering how one of us had, yet again, survived a visit to the local hospital.

The place of my birth, Yorkshire, is renowned for its steep inclines and we would take full advantage of these tailor-made hills to road test whichever homemade go-kart we had patched together. Two sets of pram wheels would be the main requirement. Big ones at the back and small ones at the front with two footholds at the front for whichever one of us felt brave enough to hold the steering together with their feet whilst clutching some tied-up rope with their hands.

These contraptions, assembled together with an

assortment of wood sections, would be capable of going from 0 to 60mph in about 20 seconds, and as we accelerated past the local shops the owners would be rushing out to get their wares inside for fear that we would crash into them. These dragsters had no semblance of any braking system at all and most definitely no parachute coming out of the back once we had reached our maximum speed; it was inevitable that at some stage we would either be hitting the roadside kerb and spilling out in all directions, or ultimately our final resting place would be the wall at the end of the journey that we would all be catapulted into.

The karts were only capable of carrying two of us children at a time and after each excursion the speedster would need pulling all the way back to the crest of the hill. This would be very time consuming and would frustrate the other children who waited patiently for their turn. The situation would often be resolved by upwards of four of us cramming onto the kart together as tightly as possible, with not an inch to spare and even the slight bit of steering, possible with a one-man unit, would now be out of the question.

All of us would have known the inevitable outcome as we gathered more and more momentum, as we raced through to the inevitable outcome of crashing head-on into whichever wall we were destined to hit. After an acceptable period of concussion from one or more of us we would simply roar with laughter and set about hauling the kart back up the hill for a repair job, and once completed, yet another excursion down the hill. Jack and Jill or Humpty Dumpty didn't have a patch on the bumps, abrasions, and cracked heads of my small gang.

We were proper street urchins who maybe saw soap and water twice a week, and maybe a good strip wash on a Sunday in a tin bath in preparation for school the following day.

We were very inventive in my youth and parents would welcome us staying out for long periods due to the lack of entertainment within the home, but many of our activities would give modern-day health and safety representatives nightmares as we took our life in our own hands most days. I do believe in the adage "we had nothing but we were happier then" because much of our fun would be spent outdoors, whereas modern-day children finish school and retreat to their rooms to enter some strange cyber world of computers. I would rather have my childhood and I'm sure many feel the same if they are honest.

We would march to other Protestant areas, or to other gangs' neighbourhoods, carrying dustbin lids as shields and house bricks to throw at our opponents, and yet again the local casualty department would have to be preparing stitches for one of us with the dreaded question all of us feared as children: "When did you last have your tetanus jab?" That one question would have me racing for the exit on many an occasion.

Obviously some of the parents would soon prefer their offspring to be much safer by not associating with me for whatever reason, which would be a wise decision in hindsight because in later years some of those same boys would spend spells in borstals or prisons with me. None of us could have envisaged what lay ahead because for now we were far too busy just being children.

On one adventure to an apple and pear orchard we had "scrumped" on many an occasion, we needed to take an alternative route in because the owners had set a series of tripwire traps to make them aware when someone was in their very huge garden. The decision was made to scale down a very large wall and with bags in hand we proceeded to fill them at speed and get back up the wall much quicker than we had come down due to the alarm being raised. After many finger holds and an exhausting climb, once again laughing, we realised one of our gang, Sydney, was not amongst us.

We made our way back to the estate anticipating trouble with our parents should the police become involved, but to our surprise there were no long-winded lectures forthcoming and normal activities would be resumed.

When any one of us would call for Sydney we would be told abruptly that he was unwell and would not be playing out for the foreseeable future.

It was not until a later date we found out that two gay men lived in one of the flats close to the orchard and had taken Sydney back, tied him up, and made him perform disgusting sexual acts on them resulting in them both being sent to prison for lengthy terms. It certainly put us off stealing apples for a while, the rewards seemed not to match the dangers.

I never saw Sydney for many years and when I did on the odd occasion, he would understandably prefer not to discuss that day and what happened to him, and I would not press him on the matter. I would always be thankful that I was able to scale that wall far quicker than he had.

I had taken a paper job in which I had to deliver newspapers around the estate, but it also gave me the opportunity to steal and place things in my big hessian bag which I did on many occasions. That bag became perfect cover for me to steal things on numerous occasions because I had it with me most of the time. The licensing hours around this time deemed that premises shut during the day and then re-open at 5.30pm. I would be required to deliver an evening newspaper to the local working men's club, which would be empty and the shutters down in the bar. I had discovered on an earlier visit that if I slammed the palms of my hands onto the shutters and pressed hard they would rise, giving me the chance to hop over the bar and help myself to bottles of beer and cigarettes. I would then hop back over the bar and shutters would be replaced in an instant, and then make my way down onto the railway tracks where I had discovered a disused air raid shelter built into the embankment.

My ill-gotten gains would then be concealed here to share with my little gang as this had become our secret little headquarters where we smoked, drank, played cards, and all of the other things that good Catholic kids did. We had straw on the floor and over a period of time put chairs and rolls of linoleum in and set about hiding it from view.

About this time one or two of the girls would also play truant from school, and although I had sworn the lads to secrecy I made the foolish decision to take one of the girls back to the shelter.

I had never had sex before but had become curious and had chosen a very overweight girl for fear of making a fool of myself. Of course I remember the girl's name but feel that it would be ungentlemanly of me to mention her name here.

I did not have much of a clue what I was doing as I fumbled about, but fortunately the girl of my desire had previous experience and after a little frothing at the mouth by yours truly, the deed was done and for the next few weeks I walked about with an added spring in my step.

It did not go down too well that I chose to ignore the girl from thereon, and if I am honest I practically snubbed her, believing I now had much juicier fruit to feed upon. Not the most satisfactory conclusion to my first sexual encounter, but who amongst us found that very first time a truly moving and romantic experience? Even the setting left a lot to be desired – a disused air raid shelter with straw on the floor wouldn't be a lasting memory for anyone.

The lady in question did not take too kindly to being snubbed and wasted no time in telling everyone about my little Aladdin's cave of stolen goods, until eventually the gossip reached the ears of the local constabulary and I would be the recipient of quite a few clips around the ear both at the station and at my family home. Needless to say I was now made redundant from my newspaper round and in need of another source of income.

While we would walk to school a couple of aging sisters used to sell all of the schoolchildren loose cigarettes at exorbitant prices, or buy cigarette coupons from the children to purchase items from a catalogue. These sisters had no qualms about selling "loosies" to whatever age group and the decision was taken to observe and try to gauge just exactly where the proceeds were hidden, which seemed to be a shoe box on top of a shelf within the pantry in the kitchen.

My friend and I went in and whilst he kept one of the sisters occupied buying cigarettes. I crept to the pantry and once the shoe box was safely tucked under my arm, sprinted from the kitchen, spilling some of the contents while I did so, albeit only the loose change. My friend was detained by the sisters for a while until finally believing his protestations that he did not know me and he had become an innocent witness to the actions. It mattered little to me, the action I had just taken.

I never felt much remorse about anything I did at that time and I was more than confident the police would not be involved, because both of the sisters would need to explain their own actions.

My friend and I would share out the proceeds of the princely sum of seventeen pounds, not exactly a king's ransom but adequate enough for two people of our tender years.

I threw the bundle of cigarette coupons in the first bin I came across because they were of no use to me, and on the off chance that the police may become involved it would be a good indication to them that I was implicated. I could never understand the logic back then that people would smoke thousands of cigarettes and need to save an enormous amount of coupons to exchange for something as petty as an ironing board or a kettle, but there was a little consolation for the sisters as they would not be doing much ironing for a while.

My logic may seem a little harsh but these pair weren't exactly pillars of society.

Throughout my life I have committed various crimes but I can honestly say, hand on heart, I have never at any time burgled from a dwelling house where ordinary working-class people live.

Admittedly in a lot of your eyes it would not make a lot of difference, but to many of us who became criminals, a lot of us have certain codes of conduct and we don't stray from that.

As I have stated earlier, it's circumstances that dictate what we become, and that's not to say every poor child becomes a law breaker, but me personally, I never once regretted what I was doing. I always seemed to have money from one source or the other and my world was comfortable. Some weeks I would probably have more in my pockets than my father who had worked all week, and that was despite the fact we were basically still children and at times immature.

A local greengrocer had moved out of his corner shop and it had long been rumoured on the estate that the owner had a hand grenade and a German helmet in the shop. A story passed down year after year with a little added each time until some of the others had even seen the helmet and the grenade. Looking back, it's funny now what you believe in your mind's eye as children, and God knows what I thought I was going to do with one had it existed. It doesn't bear thinking about. I would have possibly attempted to blow my school up in one of my many rebellious moods.

Once the owner moved out and into a recently

built shopping complex and left behind all sorts of oddments, I decided to smash a few windows and enter the premises to have a little forage around.

No grenade was to be found I'm afraid, but as I tore the units away from the wall in the offices a brown paper parcel tied with string dropped to the floor, and the contents of this package was an extremely large amount of money, hidden away many years before because it certainly didn't belong to the previous owner of the shop.

Along with the money were a few pieces of jewellery, which I simply threw away over the neighbouring church wall. On reflection, the jewellery would have been expensive items but I cared little for the shiny things, leave them for the magpies.

I was throwing bundles of money up into the air and shared some of my newfound wealth amongst some of my trusted friends on the estate. It was quite a bit of money, was £800 at this period in time, and was proving difficult to spend, but it was fun attempting to do so.

I had begun to hang around with some of the local Hell's Angels by now, in the local bus station, and I gave one of them £100 towards a bike. I was in my early teens and had long since given up on religion and especially redemption.

I had accepted I had turned into a "bad sort" and I had no intention of changing. One or two had already suggested that prison would straighten me out. I doubted that very much and the time was fast approaching when we would all get the chance to see if it was I or they who was correct.

Imprisonment was beckoning!!!!

CHAPTER 4

My childhood was seeming to be over in the blink of an eye really, but I have lots of fond memories from that time. There was lots of poverty about and a lot of hungry kids. It's ok having Catholic beliefs about contraception but the more mouths there are that need feeding, the less food there is on the table. Given all that though, I would still rather have been born into poverty rather than wealth. It's possible to learn much more about the person you are likely to become whilst languishing at the bottom of the pile. But for now, more pressing matters lay at hand.

Because of the large amount of money from the "burglary" of an empty shop, the local CID had begun to take an interest in me and I was about to be on a head-on collision course with them which would turn me against the police for the remainder of my life and still to this day.

The head of this branch at that time was a man called Donald Hirst, who I am sure many of Dewsbury's criminal fraternity will remember with a bad taste in their mouths. I had already hidden a great deal of the money and no way would I be parting with it very easily. My sister had given some carol singers far more than she should have in the run-up to Christmas and awkward questions had begun to be asked. Obviously the previous shopkeeper had been interviewed and he must have just clutched at a figure out of the blue and claimed the package had contained £250. This confirmed what I already believed, that the money certainly was not his.

Now in situations like this, it's the time that corrupt police officers rise to the surface as scum does on a polluted river. They are suddenly aware money is there for the taking with no one in particular able to question matters. Donald Hirst and a fellow crooked colleague paid a friendly visit to my grandmother's house, exchanging pleasantries after assuring her he just wanted me to accompany them and show my point of entry to the burgled premises. Alarm bells should have rung when they showed up in an old style white police dog van and I was placed in the back whilst they both sat in the front. Once out of earshot of my grandmother they both made it clear in no uncertain terms that they wished to know where the money was by the time they found a secluded area, or they would be coming in the back for a more "physical conversation".

Over and over I insisted that the shopkeeper was

correct with the figure of £250, but they insisted I was lying and on parking up, the fat detective that was Donald Hirst got hold of me by the hair and throat in the back of the van and gave me several slaps and punches. Many of you may feel that because of the lifestyle I was leading the beating was a little deserved, but I have lived in this setting for many years now and can assure you that these two gentlemen had no interest in solving any crime.

Had I not been strong willed and gave this pair the slightest indication where the money could be located, there is no way that money would have been handed into any police station. These pair were just after a quick little earner on the side for themselves with absolutely no comeback at all. Any complaints I should choose to make would simply fall on deaf ears.

So I had met the leader of the pack, "The Don", the so-called legend of the force that was Donald Hirst who in actual fact turned out to be just as much a criminal as myself. Be upstanding for the pillars of society, the upholders of law and order. Battle lines had been drawn now and I had a burning hatred for this man and his colleague. I had also learnt a valuable lesson that in most instances there is not a lot of difference between us and them.

We would meet many times over the next few years but he must have known in his heart that if he couldn't intimidate me in my younger years in the back of that van, he would have little or no chance as I became older and wiser. Maybe it was meeting these sort of individuals and crossing swords that brought that little excitement into my life that I craved. I'd already been a shady little bastard for a long while now but to get one over on any of these bigger bastards had now set me on the path of becoming a career criminal.

I would burgle many premises that were of a business nature and by now had met many older criminals who had quickly given me their seal of approval as a lad who could be trusted and certainly was not a grass. One of my proudest achievements in life is that I have never even been the cause of another man spending even one day in a prison cell, let alone serving a sentence.

I began to spend more and more time with the Hell's Angels in Dewsbury bus station and many things that I stole could always be sold on through my contacts with the bikers. One of them, named Jesus, became a particularly close friend and a person who I would spend a lot of time with. His true name as Alan Sheard and while I was serving a prison sentence a few years later the sad news came through on the radio that Jesus had been stabbed to death with a bayonet at a big gathering of Hell's Angels in Normanton, which is close to Wakefield.

I've lost many friends over the years and many of them in violent situations far removed from normal everyday life, but I took Alan's death really badly because he gave me a lot of guidance for that period I was around him. Don't get me wrong, I would still be off the rails at times, but Alan would always reason with me and try to keep me calm. Occasionally we would end up in fist fights with the local mods and scooterists who used to meet at a northern soul club called the BinLid at the back of one of the local cinemas. After one very heated fracas and one or two of the bikers getting hurt, I took it upon myself to teach them a lesson once their club closed. I stacked all of the dustbins on the side street up against the doors of the BinLid club and proceeded to set one or two of them alight until the contents began to lick flames up the door and melted all of the plastic signs above it.

I made myself scarce but on the next occasion I met Jesus he gave me a very stern lecture. I had always been a thief of sorts but he explained to me the enormity of an arson attack, which could leave me serving a very long sentence. He was a good man and a sort of father figure to me, and I felt I betrayed him a lot when I changed fashions myself a few years down the way and I could be seen astride scooters and wearing all of the latest mod clothes.

We all have those transitional periods in our life where we have a sort of identity crisis while we struggle to discover who we are and what we are about.

I had worn the studded leather jackets and had hair down to my arse, but now I had my hair cropped short with partings shaved in the sides and felt really clean, fresh, and sharp when I dressed to go out. It just happened and seemed the natural thing to do, and I liked the company I was keeping, plus I had the added opportunity of having a ready-made market for when I broke into the local fashion shops.

Most people then would have suits made to measure and pay weekly, and I would also need to do the same, but all of that would be done by John Laing, the bespoke tailor of that period.

Other shops in and around the town would stock

Ben Sherman, Jaytex, Brutus, or other button down shirts. They would also stock Levi and Wrangler jeans and it would take little effort to get into the back of these shops and carry away as much stock as was possible. Happy days indeed because these items would be eagerly accepted by customers willing to pay half of the retail price.

I would always be at the top of Dewsbury Police's "hot ones to question list", but I would always be prepared for this and would never have kept even one item from any burglary to keep myself at arm's length. I would have money from the proceeds of the crime to purchase clothes from different shops. Oh, the police would know it was me, but proving it would be a different matter.

At this time, I would be the first to admit I was my own little mini crime wave and burglary figures would go through the roof when I was active. There was barely a day would go by without me being involved in some crime. I had gone through a lot in my personal life by now and each time I reflect on those matters it opens up wounds I find difficult to deal with. It has caused me to be treated for clinical depression my whole life and the situation never becomes any easier.

I previously wrote a book called *Wellies & Warders* which instantly became a best seller and gives in great detail many accounts within it as to why my life spiralled out of control. I found myself all alone in the world and to be truthful, relished committing the crimes I did and in my mind imagined DS Donald Hirst getting many dressing downs from his superior for the high crime rate in the area, and that thought alone was enough to make me go out each night with gloves, screwdriver, and crowbar – I was to get my comeuppance very shortly. I wouldn't be allowed to rule the roost for very much longer. I wasn't exactly public enemy number one but I needed to be taken down a peg or two.

I would know and recognise, by now instantly, the detectives' cars who would always have two civilian policemen in them; every criminal will tell you they can be spotted a mile off and I would be off and away and up the side streets, making it impossible for the cars to follow and for sure none of them on foot at that time could get within 100 yards of me.

I had certainly had a good run but I was almost just as sure that my days were numbered and a set of handcuffs would be placed on me – but until then let the party resume and enjoy the ride.

CHAPTER 5

It wasn't as if I didn't have the same dreams and aspirations as some of the other kids, such as being a fireman or train driver, but by now the die had been cast and I didn't seem to be able to break the mould.

Incidentally, congratulations to the few school friends who perhaps really did manage to become a train driver, as their wages in the present day are even greater than major politicians, it is rumoured. Now there's a reason to hoot your horn if ever there was one.

Don't get me wrong, because I had tried a succession of jobs to keep me on the level but just found them to be mundane and soul destroying and very much underpaid. Try sitting in a woodyard and having mountain after mountain of roofing timbers stacked beside you – my objective would be to level all of the six inch nails out by hand until the timber was adequate to go through the saw mill without damaging the blades. Splinters is the term, I believe, although my grandmother's Yorkshire term would be "spelks" – the name mattered little.

What did matter was my poor hands would be full of these tiny pieces of wood, more and more at the end of each shift and the pain would be unbearable, although not as unbearable as the pittance we were paid.

I was born in a small northern mill town and most employment would revolve around these mills, unemployment would be practically unheard of. It would be possible to have three jobs within a week should you choose to do so, as jobs were in such abundance.

Benefit offices then would require you to sign at one counter and then proceed to another to be paid in cash. Nobody would be signing on for very long because card after card would be thrust into one's hand giving details of that particular week's "wonderful" job opportunities, and before you could make even the slightest excuse an appointment for an interview would have been arranged. Whenever the odd rise in unemployment did come about these dole offices soon had to rethink their strategy, as offices around the country were targeted in armed robberies due to the amount of ready cash being on hand with little or no resistance.

Outside these buildings it would also be possible to be approached by any number of "employers" who would have work available by way of cash in hand and no questions asked as a way of supplementing the unemployment benefit.

It was on one of these occasions I met what I can only describe as two of the biggest confidence tricksters I am ever likely to meet. I would not give out the names of these two because I am sure they will, even now, still be pulling one stroke or another. The bare-faced cheek of these two characters had to be seen to be believed and on regular occasions I look back and absolutely roar with laughter. One prime example I will give you:

The stage is set and plans are afoot to employ ten able-bodied men from outside the unemployment exchange; I became one of the ten. A figure of fifteen pounds per person per day was agreed. A reasonable amount of money in the day, I might add, and especially for a young boy such as myself. The job entailed demolition of a nearby disused church. We were transported to our place of work and given the instructions of how to go about our work.

There were two trucks in attendance. One would be responsible for taking away hard core rubble and the other would handle the more expensive old slating and stone and was actually where the interest in this job lay.

The two employers would strut about with clipboards, giving the appearance of being very official whilst giving out instructions.

All of this was taking place by a very busy main road and in the eyes of the general public passing by, but to all intents and purposes it would all look completely above board. In actual fact it was all a complete scam and not one person had permission to be on that site, let alone be demolishing it.

Picture the scene if you can.

No one need show any sign of nervousness because the workforce are all under the impression they are doing an honest day's work. The only people in the know were the driver and the two men in suits with clipboards, who had nerves of steel and remained composed throughout.

Police cars would drive past but not one flicker of emotion would be shown from these pair or tricksters. Years later when the filth came out I would call this pair "Butch" and "Sundance" after Butch Cassidy and the Sundance Kid.

I would be involved in many more escapades with these two men over the years once they recognised that I was also a shady little bastard, but one who could be trusted.

But for now, the job in hand; these two would always have their transport close at hand and I suppose that should it have ever even looked like awkward questions would be on the horizon, they would vacate the area immediately. It never happened and years later they informed me they had made a very handsome profit.

We would laugh at the thought of any of the men, including myself, being asked to explain just what we were doing on the premises at the time and all of us looking around for our employers to explain and display the paperwork. Butch and Sundance had a gift for this sort of thing and would also uproot mile after mile of disused railway lines and sidings using the same old tried and tested terms of employment. I would meet up with them at odd times in public houses or occasionally in prison exercise yards.

You could never meet a more colourful pair of characters and you would be hard pressed to ever convince them that they were in any shape or form criminals. I understood their logic, although I am sure many would not.

They did not class themselves as criminals and believed their actions to be innocent subterfuge with no victim. I never tired of listening to their exploits and I imagine even the magistrates or judges they came in front of would secretly smile in their chambers.

I was glad I met them at that moment in time but once the demolition of the church came to an end and nothing remained but the shell, I would once again be at a loose end and would return to burglary of shops and business properties.

Although I had, and still do have a fear of heights, it would not stop me going onto rooftops in shopping precincts to gain access to any number of shops. I may have had a fear of heights but I had a bigger fear of waking the following morning with no money and being unable to feed myself, so the fear factor needed to be overcome because rich pickings would be available in many of the town centre shops in these arcades.

I can remember a particularly big brand name at the time being "House of Fraser" and they had a very big store with three floors. Gaining access to this store involved me diving out from a ledge up the side of the building and making contact with a staircase of metal which was the fire escape. Upon making contact the staircase would drop to the ground floor.

I would then scale the staircase, break a window and access the building, and then pull it back up to its original resting place, giving the impression nothing was untoward.

The jump to make contact would be precarious and very much a leap of faith considering the fifteen foot drop below, but if it is the only access then the jump and leap must indeed be taken. Once inside I went from floor to floor and emptied the till on each floor, but it was only small amounts of change as such, and a "float" for the opening of the store early the next morning.

I knew the police made regular patrols on foot of these areas because I had watched them many times while I loitered about on the nearby market stalls. The store was littered with many dressed mannequins displaying styles the ladies were wearing during that period in time.

For fear of me being spotted by police or other passers-by while I was in the shop, I donned a ladies' winter coat, a string of fake pearls, and a sort of summer hat with a ribbon around the brim. I dread to think what I must have looked like at the time but I was confident that should anyone look through the window, I could freeze in an instant and blend in with the other figures in the shop.

Many of my friends, on hearing the above anecdote, laugh and accuse me of being a cross dressing burglar, but I can assure you all nothing sexual was involved in my play even though I may have looked rather pretty, ha ha.

My biggest fear of that night would have been

getting caught and DS Donald Hirst being on duty, as I am sure he would have been more than insistent I wore my shop outfit into the courtroom the following day to address the magistrates. I would only need to be cautious on the ground floor because the two upper floors would be out of sight.

I searched throughout the night for what I believed to be some hidden alcove with the day's takings, but all to no avail. Upon burgling premises, I would often stay in overnight because at that time I had been homeless for a good period of time. On these occasions vigilance would be important because to fall asleep could be a fatal error considering early morning cleaners could be entering the building.

I would usually find the ideal time to vacate would be just before 6.00am when the local constabulary would be busy changing shifts, and I would look less suspicious on the streets as it would seem I was simply making my way to work. Not that I burgle anymore nowadays, but I would imagine the same principles apply to the present-day burglar.

The need, really, is to come out of one of those burglaries with a substantial amount of money, thereby cancelling out the need to repeat the procedure within a few days, because a cat may have nine lives but a burglar certainly doesn't and my wings were about to be clipped yet again.

There was a café ran by Pakistanis on a busy intersection by Bradford Road in Dewsbury, and it also had quite a lot of slot and pinball machines. I knew this because I used to frequent the place many times when I truanted from school, and this place certainly owed me quite a few shillings. I scaled a wall at the rear by the canal which, again, was a little high risk being as how I could not swim and one slip and I would have been in the water. There had to be safer jobs than this, I used to think, but my night would get much worse as it progressed.

I broke a small window, muffling the sound with my coat pressed tightly against it, and eased myself in. I forced my way into the cash box on a few of the machines and I had begun to amass quite a stack of coins when I thought I heard a noise from above the café, but I dismissed it as I knew the café had no living quarters. I took one of my socks off and proceeded by placing the assembled coins inside of it and set about acquiring myself a few more from yet another machine, when I became aware of people in the room, and in broken English I was called a "bloody bastard" and taken off my feet by a sharp blow to the head.

By now I realised two Pakistani men and an English female, all in a state of undress, were in the room. I thought maybe if I took a beating that the police would not be involved but the proprietor opened the front door of the café, shouting for assistance.

As and when he came back in the shop the three of them would scramble about trying to get dressed, although each time one of them came by me I would receive a kick or a punch. It was obvious what the three of them were up to and the female was screaming for one of them to get her clothes before the police arrived, and one of her earlier "lovers" left the room to go upstairs. While the other one was distracted trying to placate her I jumped to my feet, gave him a much heavier punch than he had given me and put him down, and made for the door in an instant.

On reflection, I possibly even had time to give the "lady" a peck on the cheek and a little pat on one of her naked buttocks, but I thought it wiser not to and made my escape as hastily as I could. Unfortunately, police presence was in the area. I had run in the wrong direction and the long arm of the law was waiting; rather than shout as they do in the movies, "You'll never take me alive, copper!" it was a meek and mild, "Ok, it's a fair cop and I'll come quietly."

The cell block at the town hall was my next port of call and if any of you have been in any cell block you will know the one blanket issued will either cover your head and not your feet or vice versa.

Well this story would be even a little colder due to the fact my socks had been confiscated as means of evidence. I had seen the last of them and the money they held in coins.

I would be held to appear at the next sitting of the magistrates but none of this held any fears for me, as I had been in this exact same situation on many occasions before.

CHAPTER 6

If I remember correctly I was sentenced to six months on that occasion. I had been in the system a few times before which makes it a little easier coming to terms with any sentence thrown at you. One problem then was no different to any other with regards to overcrowding, and three inmates would be crammed into every cell.

Many of you may feel that we all reap what we sow but to have to defecate in a bucket in the corner of the cell is inhumane if we are to be truthful. I had already endured this practice on previous sentences so it wasn't entirely unexpected or surprising that nothing much had changed. A detailed history of myself is explained in my previous book and my psychiatrist feels I released many skeletons whilst writing of that period of my life; it has been a little detrimental to my health and would be better left alone.

The brutal honesty of it is what made my book a best seller, but I readily agree that mentality created new issues for me and my medication was increased.

To briefly recap, I find myself abandoned as a small baby by my birth mother. I find myself homeless and on the streets in London, and the people who brought me up from a baby, my father and grandmother, both die within quick succession of each other and I am left alone in the world to fend for myself. A pattern soon developed and I would be the first to admit that I became institutionalised, but much worse than that, I really did not give a shit about a system that did nothing to improve my life.

I may seem rather flippant about some of the crimes I committed and the belief there is no victimless crime. That may be the case, although I also feel individuals can be victims of circumstances in our defence. Would I have turned out to be the habitual criminal I became if my figureheads in life had not died at the tender age I was?

Yes, I was already involved in a lot of petty thefts, but even so, the possibility could have been there for me to outgrow that period just as many do. But to suddenly be placed in a cycle of constant and routine imprisonment with neither visits nor correspondence forthcoming, is to be placed in a situation where you have nothing to rely on but the people around you, who are seasoned criminals.

What hope did I really have?

Some critics of the last book suggest there is a lot of self-pity, but I resent that criticism because it's a load of opinionated rubbish. All who know me will inform you I am a reasonably well-balanced individual who ultimately turned out to be a good and generous member of society who always puts others first. To gain that sort of balance requires many years of patience, reasoning, and understanding. Wisdom and gaining it is the saviour of each and every one of us but in no way will I apologise for my actions during my childhood and teen years and beyond.

Life is a learning process and if a misspent youth means spending years in institutions, then the lessons you learn therein are unlikely to be very beneficial, I'm afraid, and I really did learn more about crime than I did rehabilitation. Without intending to, I was caught up in the web of the system.

I would often feel my only option to survive would be to commit further crimes. Even within a prison, crime is prevalent. While you observe corrupt prison officers bringing in illicit drugs, alcohol, or tobacco, what hope is there really for any of the inmates in that jail?

It would be no different in any jail I was interred in, and in actual fact the same corruption will still take place in present-day prisons, albeit with the introduction of mobile phones being brought in by the prison officers.

The profit margins inside a prison are astronomical in comparison to the same deals outside of prison, and everyone has their noses in the trough unfortunately. The system will always be rotten to the core and the one thing I am happy about is that I no longer have to witness these actions.

I would feel sorry for many of the other prisoners who were also in there due to unfortunate circumstances, and especially the few at that time who found themselves in a prison although it was patently obvious they required medical accommodation. It would not be available to them due to overcrowding but the people I witnessed were extreme emergencies. They would be easily identifiable by their behavioural problems.

One would walk around the exercise yard and the smell would be unbearable, and all of the bottoms of legs and shoes could clearly be seen to be finished with faeces. People such as this would make no effort to clean themselves and the warders would feel that it wasn't their responsibility to take matters into their own hands; the situation worsened each week.

Another inmate called Leonard but nicknamed "Buff" was always trying to come out of his cell naked. Hence the nickname "Buff", I presume. On a good day though, Leonard would come out of his cell fully clothed and his coat would be emblazoned with milk bottle tops and other oddments which represented his military achievements in his mind. He would be seen constantly saluting some imaginary officer out on the exercise yard.

I had no doubt, due to his age, that at some time in his past history Leonard would have had a military career, and also would have been awarded medals.

I found it disgusting that these men should be languishing anywhere in a prison without the slightest hint of any medical care or attention, but it would be futile me registering any complaint of sorts because that would only bring the nasty-minded officers to my door.

I had many occasions when I overstepped the mark and got myself some very brutal beatings, but on the whole it was wise to quickly gather that the best bet in a prison is to keep your mouth shut, don't cause ripples, and never ever criticise officers if the likelihood is that they will be informed of who the actual complainant is.

For any of you who believe prisons are holiday camps, you are very much misinformed.

Bullying is rife, both from the inmates and the officers.

One of the hardest things to come to terms with in any prison is who you actually end up sharing a cell with, bearing in mind the confined space you are sharing between the three of you, and that arguments and fist fights are an everyday occurrence. Should you have a friend from the outside world within the jail and a reasonable officer on duty who can be bothered doing the paperwork, then it is possible to be sharing with close friends, but even then, arguments with each other can surface.

It's a very stressful existence, to be honest, and on one of these occasions I found myself in Armley prison in Leeds with some cocksure West Indian who claimed to be in for "pimping" and seemed to be proud of the fact. I was unsure what "pimping" was until a friend of mine on the exercise yard informed me it was living off immoral earnings, which namely was having young girls sleep with the punters while the pimp beat the women and took the money.

I was still young and innocent, but the tariff at that time for that particular offence would be a minimum sentence of five years' imprisonment, my friend informed me, and once I checked his card when I got back on the landing he was serving a sentence of five years and nine months.

I did not like anything about him or his manner as he strutted around the cell like a peacock and definitely liked the sound of his own voice, which in a way was good for him because I had no inclination to converse with him in any shape or form.

I had told the other inmate in the cell with us that I was about to teach this poncey twat a lesson to gauge exactly where he stood, should matters take a turn for the worse. He confirmed to me that he did not like too much about him either. I would await my moment and preferred an argument developing before I did what I intended to do.

We would be fed by a metal tray consisting of three sections for a main course, a dessert, and a hot drink. It took the Home Office years to take these trays out of circulation which always baffled me because these items were heavy duty weapons in the wrong hands and I had already witnessed many assaults take place with them. The argument did not take long to develop as Mister Hot Shot picked up the tobacco on his table that did not belong to him.

These sorts of incidents always take place to test how far someone can go in the pecking order, and usually to determine who is the cock of the walk. Should anyone ever allow this to happen unchallenged, then none of their possessions will be safe again as the bullying will increase.

I had waited for this moment to come, and it had

come much quicker than I thought, but I was prepared. After telling him to put the tobacco back in its rightful place and him smiling in a sneering manner and simply continuing to do what he had started to do, I jumped from the bed swiftly and in the one movement, brought the metal tray into full contact with his mouth, drawing blood instantly.

I have never witnessed someone curl into a defensive corner on the floor as quickly as this person did, and all of his earlier bravado had left him while he squealed for mercy. I imagined that this was exactly the same scenario some of his ladies of the night had to endure from the bully.

I put the tray down once I realised he was putting up no resistance but I still gave him the odd kick to keep him on the defensive. When he got the opportunity he pressed the panic button in the cell until a warder came and opened the door.

He gave his version of events, and me and the other cellmate gave ours, and the officer just told him to collect his personal things. It isn't like a furniture removal van is needed in a prison, and he was gone within minutes and moved to another cell where no doubt he would get yet another slap.

Before the warder closed the door he gave us a knowing wink as if to say, "I realise what all this is about and there won't be any more recriminations."

Obviously he needed a few stitches around his mouth but I'd presume he had doled out the same treatment, albeit to women.

He would see me regularly on the exercise yard but chose to give me a very wide berth which was perhaps the right thing to do, rather than risk any further injury to himself. He had been in such haste to leave our cell that he had not noticed I had put his tobacco in my own pocket, and it wasn't like he was going to return asking for it. Hopefully he was taught a lesson in life at that moment, although I very much doubt it.

My remaining cellmate was a little bit nervous around me, having just witnessed the level of violence he had just seen, but normality was soon resumed once he realised he had additional tobacco rations to get him through the week as I shared out the spoils of our recent lodger.

I was never then and nor am I now even the slightest bit of a bully.

But if an individual needs putting in his place I am usually capable of doing it and especially if I have the additional bonus of a weapon at hand.

I was getting to reach the stage where I enjoyed the violence though, which caused me a little concern, but not enough to attempt to curb it.

The sentence soon passed and I found myself back on the streets of Dewsbury with the £25.00 discharge grant in my pocket, but once again nowhere to live and alone on the streets.

But hey-ho! These things are sent to test us and we either sink or swim.

I was out and I needed a beer and some recreational drugs, so deal with one problem at a time for now.

CHAPTER 7

Throughout my life I spent the best part of eleven years in one institution or another and on each occasion I was discharged I would come out with all of the best intentions in the world. A new beginning, a fresh start. But the reality is that it is difficult to do so, and being a homeless teenager, it would become increasingly difficult.

Firstly, I would need to sign on at the employment exchange and being as how I had to do so with a "no fixed abode" status, it caused major problems. This particular way of signing on requires a daily signing, therefore ensuring that you are not repeating the same procedure in other towns across the area. On each day I signed I would be given a payment of £1.50 and on a Friday an additional payment of £4.50 to cover the weekend costs – I kid you not.

I think the assumption was that 50p per meal per day was more than sufficient.

Many others were in the same situation at the time and a local café in Dewsbury bus station called the Bon Bon would be a familiar meeting place. The Greek owner would take sympathy on some of the younger ones such as myself and occasionally give out a free plate of chips and the odd tea or coffee.

Hunger is one of the worst feelings to ever have and until you have eaten from a bin through pure situation, you would not begin to appreciate that. Whilst some would loiter in the café throughout the day for warmth more than anything, there would also be the odd opportunity to get a little "casual" employment with cash-in-hand payments to supplement the dole money.

Any number of employers would pop their heads through the door in search of able-bodied men/women to deliver leaflets or become furniture removal men for the day. This has always been the way of the world and throughout time the need for a short-term workforce will always exist.

Whatever and wherever the job was, it would need to be completed by a certain deadline to ensure being available to sign on at the given time.

Eventually I acquired a job with daily wages on a very regular basis, but it involved travelling over into Lancashire posting the standard bin bag with accompanying leaflets detailing the charitable work we were doing with anything donated.

It was for a company called Plaistree and Hangor and was very much above board and not at all like the bogus collectors of today. The job would entail posting thousands of these bags one morning and in the afternoon, collecting the ones posted the previous morning. We would have a big van to do so and on the return journey we would drive back, albeit with a couple of us lads in the back of the van rummaging through some of the bags to find something half decent to wear.

We would not feel this was out of order in any way considering we had walked miles and miles throughout our shift, and if anything, some of us were charity cases.

I still could not resist being involved in anything a little shady and I suppose I could have settled for my daily wages, but I felt I had gone without and struggled for long enough and so took the decision to pull another stroke I had recently learned about.

I went and got myself a room at the local bed and breakfast hotel ran by an old dear called Annie Skettington.

Mrs Skettington wrote me a letter confirming to the unemployment office that I would be residing at her abode for the foreseeable future and she required two weeks' board and lodgings in advance.

The lady and I got on because I regard myself as quite an amiable character and she enjoyed having the banter with me. I had carefully laid out plans and I told her that it may only be temporary as I had possibilities of working away very soon. Once the first payment arrived from the dole I duly paid the amount that was needed to the landlady and she was more than pleased. I waited a day or so and informed her the job I was waiting for had arrived and I would be leaving in the next day or so.

She was very pleased for me and wished me well and attempted to give me some of the monies back; she felt she had been overpaid. I assured her that she was a very nice lady and to treat herself because I wouldn't be saying anything to the authorities.

Stage two is now required.

I visited the Social Security who had made the payment and voiced my fears that I was fortunate to receive the payment because some very unsavoury characters lived within the household and also had access to the incoming mail. I informed them it would be much better that I received my payment by way of Personal Issue. This required picking it up at the office over the counter once a week.

They thanked me for notifying them and appreciated my "honesty" which I had to laugh at inwardly. The end result being I could go to my charity job daily, except on a Friday, when I would go and collect a giro with a payment for one of the most expensive boarding houses, and my days were happy and my pockets would be full.

It may seem a little greedy but was that not the same as the landlady stuffing more notes into her ever-increasing purse when she had the opportunity?

No! Fuck that!

The whole world is corrupt when it wants to be and I had just been getting by and having to survive on 50p a meal for the previous few months. I have no shame in anything I did at that time because I had to live off my wits and survive. I defy any of you not to use any means at your disposal when your back is to the wall. I was a teenage boy for Christ's sake, who nobody wanted, and I had to help myself. No one was going to do it for me.

I had still left myself homeless by my actions but my place of work had a little office in a weighbridge and I would sleep in there most nights. Yes, it would be quite cold some evenings, but with all of my additional funds coming in I would be able to consume much more alcohol and once I staggered into my makeshift home in my drunken state I would soon fall asleep. I never seemed to want to live in a regular home.

I had long since been accustomed to being on the streets.

I had been alone from a very early age and although it wouldn't be a lifestyle I would recommend to everyone, it had certainly made me far more streetwise than many who were the same age as me. I find it alarming when I see friends of mine now, still living at home with their parents.

I did not need to fly the nest; my path had been set out and at times was very harsh.

I'm not sure how much it harmed me but I certainly knew it toughened me up, and so in the end it all balances itself out.

Drugs and alcohol were becoming leading players though, in my life, but I'm certain that it would be the same with everyone who lives on the streets. In life, in times of despair, we all need a crutch of sorts and I was no different.

My bigger problem was that I would display very

violent tendencies at times, but I would disregard my actions and have little sympathy for any of the victims of these outbursts.

It would trouble me a little, I suppose, but I had many mental issues and demons I was dealing with and even to this day get regular medication to just calm me down and hopefully keep me on a balanced level.

Medication only holds you down to a certain degree and I can often be found on a short fuse if I forget to take it, and violent incidents can still surface in and around me.

All of us are different and it's what makes us unique.

None of you can question my actions, to be honest.

I haven't lived in your shoes and nor have you in mine. Let him without sin cast the first stone, is the old adage.

Crime would never be far away in my life as it was all I had ever seemed to know. As stated previously, whenever I was released I would have all the best intentions but as always the inevitable conclusion would be standing in a courtroom yet again. I had no one to give me guidance and put that arm around me to give me the direction I required. Once I had been in prison on the occasions I had, then it didn't act as a deterrent, if I am to be honest. I found it all amusing and no more than another adventure.

I would never at any time conform whilst I was in there and I would often be found down in solitary confinement on some sort of punishment detail.

The only thing beneficial about and prison is the

opportunity to hone your educational skills, and I would always take advantage of the opportunity to do so.

It was always tutors who came in from the outside world to take the lessons, and I would never see them as part of the establishment, and so in turn they would have my full attention. Every time I was out I would perhaps last three months maximum before I would be locked up again. It became a vicious circle because once you have a criminal record it's a foregone conclusion that once you re-offend you are going straight back to prison.

The only question would be for how long.

The same faces would be on the reception wing or exercise yard that I had met many years before, and obviously the same problems would be reoccurring in their lives. Always in mitigation, my defense solicitor would detail this miserable existence I had endured from an early age, but to no avail. They had heard it all before on earlier occasions and I would smirk in their direction whilst waiting for the completion of all the formalities. Let's cut the bullshit and get straight to the sentence, shall we?

What's the sentence? Which prison am I going to?

I used to be bored waiting for them to return with their conclusion.

It was obvious I would be going to prison so what on earth did they do with their half-hour debate? Water the plants? Make another brew of Earl Grey?

Courtrooms and all of their pomp and pageantry and the seriousness of it all belongs in a Monty Python sketch, as far as I'm concerned. Maybe my lack of respect at times got me a bigger sentence than I would have normally received but no way would I ever bow to these people.

Obviously on reflection I now realise I did myself no favours and I would say, undoubtedly, I had a very big chip on my shoulder but I was also a very angry young man and had every right to be so.

I would often spit in their direction as I was led from any courtroom and find out at a later stage I had been given a further seven days for contempt of court. I would be told that I had the option of writing an apologetic letter to a magistrate or judge and the additional days would be waived. Kiss my arse, that would never be happening; I absolutely love writing and have spent my whole life with a pen in my hand, but never to grovel to no judge.

Dear Judge… M'lud… Please forgive my actions.

I'd rather do the seven days, if you don't mind.

My attitude would cost me jobs and place me in the very situations I was trying to avoid, or maybe I was kidding myself. I was still getting the board and lodging payments over the counter each week and it was easy enough to get through the week if I boosted it with a little shoplifting here and there.

I was by now drinking heavily and my drug consumption was through the roof. Not having a job meant I could now drink through the day as well as the evening. Fortunately, at this time the public houses used to shut in the afternoon at 3.00pm and re-open at 5.30pm.

On one of the visits to the pub I ended up with some gypsies who were just perfect for me because they said I could do some tarmacking with them on the rake, which in normal circumstances would be a hard day but with this particular gang, once the pub opened at 11.00am, the rakes would be redundant until 3.00pm when it closed again, and once we finished work it would be back to the pub.

All the wages would be spent drinking and not a lot of work would have been done to earn those wages. I could hardly understand a word they were saying a lot of the time but it would be days filled with laughter. I would have made a good traveller/gypsy type because I liked their behaviour as it was very similar to my own.

They liked to drink and they liked to fight and that was definitely my sort of lifestyle at the time. But one of these fights would soon put me back into my all too familiar place of residence.

The Big House, Her Majesty's Prison, Armley, Leeds 12.

It was time to sew mailbags for a living again.

CHAPTER 8

Same old hustle and bustle in the reception in the prison and screws with fat arses from sitting on chairs, barking out orders and trying to just intimidate the new arrivals.

It's easy to spot the first-timers who instantly just jump up and run upon hearing their names called.

Every little detail takes an age during this period, while it is confirmed who you are and what your sentence is and your religion. A doctor sees each individual for perhaps five seconds and asks, "Are you fit and well?"

It's a production line of misfits and miscreants and once all of the paperwork is complete and everyone has been formally introduced, then it's time for the next dance. Showered and fed and time to grab a bundle of previously used prison issue clothing and bedding and be escorted to your place of residence.

When entering the main hall of the prison I can hear the gasps from some of the inmates at the enormity of the place. At this stage everyone is given a landing and cell number and the letter of the wing you are to head for. This now becomes quite funny – the new ones are instantly recognisable while they wander about, all confused and disorientated. The regular reoffenders simply amble along at their own pace, knowing the destination.

When you reach your cell any prisoner will readily tell you the first thing to do is look through the spyhole and assess the calibre of the cellmates within, and you can determine if you are likely to dislike or have any problems with them. Prisons are full of liars and big fantasists and I would always choose my friends carefully and prefer people I knew and trusted from any earlier sentence.

I would rather sit in a cell with two strangers and complete silence than listen to falsehoods and bullshit all day. It could be fun to be in a cell with someone who is in for the very first time because they are eager to please everyone, and so they share what little they have.

Having said that, it can become tiresome when you are in need of sleep and yet they have a thousand more meaningless questions. In a prison it serves no purpose prolonging the day by talking well into the early hours. The quicker the day is complete and over the better.

Get to sleep at the earliest time possible and get another day ticked off.

I was now serving a two-and-a-half-year sentence

for a street robbery that went wrong, and I had stabbed someone with a sharpened steel comb. This was by far the longest sentence I had received to date at that time but it was water off a duck's back to me. I was asked if I needed to see "the Welfare" at all, and if I had any problems.

Yes, of course I've got a fucking problem – a big one. I'm stuck in this shithole for however long.

But I did not voice my concerns and politely declined his offer to see the do-gooders.

I never was one for bitching and complaining, preferring to keep any of my problems private. People who are constantly complaining about one thing or another will be constantly teased and advised to "go and see the Welfare".

The Welfare is a resident social worker who apparently tries to ensure family contact is maintained while a prisoner is inside, or deals with other issues. Great – so that ruled me right out considering I had no family.

Other prisoners would laugh each morning, already knowing it would be the very same individuals who would be lined up each day requesting to see the social worker.

These very same prisoners are usually the ones to avoid because they are so weak-willed and unable to cope. I would never suffer these fools gladly and if I was unfortunate enough to have one in the same cell constantly complaining, I would soon lose my temper and ask them to get a move to another cell.

I suffered from depression but would always try to make the best of a bad situation and rise above it.

"For fuck's sake!" I would scream. "You are in here, now deal with it." It's overwhelming for some of them and I have been in a cell where individuals actually cried themselves to sleep.

Prisons are a melting pot of all walks of society and it's not practical to be babysitting these mild-mannered individuals whilst trying to come to terms with your own situation and circumstances.

The last thing I would need while serving a lengthy sentence is some prat crying into his supper each night, trying to come to terms with his smaller sentence of a few months.

A person of this calibre needs to be with someone of a similar nature and sentence or can quite easily get hurt. Last I heard because I have not been in prison for a long while, the situation had worsened to the stage where prisons have delegated "listeners" who stay in a cell with someone overnight for fear they might commit suicide.

These are specific prisoners with a caring attitude who have been designated to do this duty after a suitable period of training – Jesus Christ, what have prisons become?

Man up and do the sentence you have been given.

Prisons have changed for the worse and Crimestoppers phone numbers on posters can be seen on walls throughout the prison to encourage some of a slyer nature to inform on others with the possibility of an earlier release.

With my violent tendencies I am sure I could not live amongst these snakes and vipers without there being an incident or confrontation.

It costs nothing to be honourable and I could not live amongst any of these present-day criminals either on the street or within a jail. But for now and my present predicament I was allocated my place of work which was sewing mail bags, which I had done on a previous sentence.

A very mundane job indeed but at least it gave some of us the opportunity to socialise with each other, have a laugh, and reminisce about what we had been up to since we last met. Prison can be a hard time or you can go with the flow and take it in your stride.

How any of you can come to the conclusion that prisons are holiday camps is beyond me.

These places are full of the most violent, volatile, and unpredictable people imaginable.

My first task in any of these places would be to make a homemade shank or any weapon that would come in handy should it be needed. Most of the chairs in the cell would be interlocking and many of them would give the appearance of being solid and in their original shape, but a leg would be off in seconds, should it be called for.

Violent incidents escalate from the slightest of incidents and although I carried a shank I would prefer not to use it, but the bottom line is, it is necessary to carry one and let it be clearly known you are no mug or you will be trodden underfoot.

Having said all of this, if one sticks to his own select circle of friends it is quite possible to avoid the madness and mayhem that takes place.

Keep the circle small and at all times watch each other's backs and it all becomes a stroll in the park to be honest. The majority of us would remain calm and laid back because of the amount of cannabis coming into the jail.

The warders would turn a blind eye to it a lot of the time and the odd one or two would even smuggle it in and sell at a very inflated price. In most prisons when a discreet phone call needs making the best person to use is the chaplain after the Sunday service.

Prisoners could approach the priest with a story of some "concern" taking place outside and the need to make a phone call then, rather than in the morning when the Welfare was available. A sympathetic ear could always be relied upon from the priest and many drug deals for impending visits would be carried out on these phone calls and without any fear of being overheard.

Any institutional system requires a few shortcuts and security is never as tight as the prison governor seems to think. A governor does not run his prison, I'm afraid. The prisoners do, and of course the few corrupt warders.

Whenever you read of prison riots and rooftop protests it usually coincides with industrial action the warders are embroiled in over their pay and conditions.

They need to portray themselves in a favourable light and bang the drum about the importance of their duties in containing very violent criminals, and what better way to express that than a major riot by the prisoners? How do you think that all of a sudden hundreds of prisoners gain access to rooftops in the first place that hitherto were inaccessible? Is security that lax? Food for thought.

Trust me, the wardens are very manipulative when they need to be and use many situations to gain themselves an unworthy status. I had little or nothing to do with many of them.

I had already amassed many stitches and broken bones from these bastards and I would never converse with them in any shape or form unless it was absolutely essential. None of them are to be trusted, not even the ones bringing in the contraband.

This sentence proved to be no different to any other as long periods of it would be spent in solitary confinement due to my attitude. I could never conform and would constantly be locking horns and playing up. It becomes a game, a battle of wills.

They drag you through the prison whilst kicking and punching you so the other prisoners can witness that this is what they can expect to endure should they also choose to want confrontation at any time.

Upon reaching the ground floor holding area usually called "The Block", I would be thrown into a cell like a dart and be expected to remain silent and cower in a corner.

This is now intended to be game over, and I am meant to have been placed firmly under their control.

But I would never yield and as soon as I could stand I urinated against the door, knowing that some of it would go under the door – checkmate.

Prisons would never keep me for too long a period before transferring me to another. I was described as a "Hot Potato" which I found quite amusing.

Occasionally I would be "Shanghaied", a term used for being given no prior warning I was about to be moved and being taken out of the cell and moved in transit within the hour.

Other more troublesome prisoners would be taken during the night and just spirited away. This action would be called "Ghosting".

It happened to plenty in my day and no doubt still occurs now.

If any prisoner gets a reputation for being disruptive then throughout that sentence the likelihood is you will be seeing the inside of many more prisons than would be the norm. It has its advantages because the normal practice is that I would be placed in many single cells as part of the punishment.

In a regular prison at this time, a shower or bath would only be permitted once a week which was very inadequate, and there was not a lot of privacy in a cell containing three prisoners. In a single cell you would be gifted the opportunity to strip wash every day really, with the only intrusion being the spyhole.

I preferred the seclusion and long peaceful days to myself.

This was my way of coming to terms with overcrowding in prisons and I would spend months at a time like this. Another bonus was that I could masturbate in peace when I had reached the stage of impossible frustration. That would never be possible in a crowded cell.

Some of my friends would be concerned for me and the amount of time I spent down "The Block" but I really didn't care. I would never cower and conform to what they deemed to be their terms and conditions.

It wasn't like I had signed a contract when I came in.

I had been given a sentence. I also had a discharge date and in my opinion anything between those periods was bullshit and I had no intention of becoming involved.

Time passes just the same and they could not hold me forever.

My time would soon come around and once again I was to be discharged with the warder's voice echoing in my ears. "You'll be back, Ginnelly."

With a quick retort of, "Fuck off, you fat cunt," I was let out onto the streets and the gates closed behind me.

No knotted brown paper parcel for me, I think that scenario is saved for the big screen or TV drama.

Off licence was needed; cigarettes, alcohol, and a train from Manchester to Dewsbury. The Trans-Pennine Express.

One of Yorkshire's own was returning home.

CHAPTER 9

Any departing prisoner will firstly be shocked in a pleasant way at the changes in fashion, but then will feast his eyes on all of the pretty girls on view. The highlight of the day will be the realisation that the train that one will be departing on is also accompanied by a buffet car.

The train journey from Manchester to Dewsbury is only a short period of perhaps forty minutes, but when you have not consumed any alcohol for the last sixteen months the buffet car is like an oasis in the desert, and lots of released prisoners will have propped many of these bars up.

Caution is needed with any alcohol consumption after a long period of abstinence because the effect hits you much more quickly. It was with this in mind I took a seat away from the bar and in one of the carriages. I sat across from some old lady who I took little notice of as the train pulled away.

After a short while, as I glanced across while I took another long swig from the can, I noticed this lady glaring through me with a look of disgust that I was consuming alcohol this early in the morning. The one thing I cannot abide is judgemental people. I had no intention of causing a scene and so I set about having a little fun to help kill the journey.

I held out the can for the lady to have a drink and obviously her disgust increased tenfold as she tried hard now to avoid eye contact. The bait had been thrown and I now had my landing net in my hand. I said to the lady that she would have to excuse my behaviour drinking this early during the day, but I had recently been released from Strangeways Prison.

I got no further with that little ice breaker because she sprang to her feet and waltzed away better than any of the competitors on Strictly Come Dancing.

People like this who live in ivory towers disgust me, if I am to be honest.

The lady knew nothing of me or my life and should rightly have had no need to look down her nose at me, but she had drawn her conclusions and that was that – no great loss to me.

The train weaved its way through Stalybridge and Miles Platting until I could smell the sweet atmosphere of Yorkshire as we arrived in Huddersfield, and I only had a short journey before we reached my hometown.

As we approached Dewsbury train station I had my head out of the carriage door looking at the familiar landscape, but I also noticed a police presence on the platform. It could have been for a totally unrelated matter but I was taking no chances and concealed myself in the toilets and decamped at the next station down the line, which was Batley, and only maybe two miles away.

When a prisoner is discharged from a prison the governor is obliged to inform the local constabulary of the impending release. I had lost that much remission for my bad behaviour that my discharge date would have been changed several times and would have caused much confusion. Prisoners can be arrested outside of the prison gates and taken into custody for previous offences committed before their imprisonment.

Police can also put in an appearance to give you their friendly warning that they know you are back and they will be observing you.

Batley offered me the same liquid refreshment that I could have got in Dewsbury anyway so it wasn't a great inconvenience. It wasn't like I had anyone to greet me or any family home with a fattened cow waiting for me. No, as always I was out on the streets but with nowhere to live – standard, really.

I had become accustomed to this sort of life for so many years previous, so it would prove to be no great hindrance to have a little sofa surf or even sleep rough.

Drugs, alcohol, and sex, and not necessarily in that order, was the next plan on the agenda after I had sharpened myself up a little and got with the present-day mode of fashion.

It was quite a smart period now, with most of the

boys wearing two-tone suits or Prince of Wales check with the customary brogues or loafers. I adored this sort of attire and always felt real sharp while I was dressed up in this manner. I would always have segs on the soles of my shoes because I enjoyed the noise they made and they would herald my arrival way before I landed.

I had taken to carrying a Stanley knife about me now and was never afraid to use it should the need arise. I was also led astray politically by the National Front who at this time were very prominent and busy targeting immigrants for shortages of housing or unemployment.

It's easy to be fuelled by this particular rhetoric when you are young and impressionable, and I am sad to say now, unfortunately I was badly influenced.

Some incidents took place which I deeply regret now and I am not prepared to go into too much detail, but all I will say in my defence is that I fortunately soon lost interest in the racist hatred these people preached. I changed direction almost as quickly as I had chosen the wrong path and in actual fact I could often be found on counter demonstrations against the National Front.

I was on a completely different side of the spectrum and would even assist in selling issues of the Socialist Workers' Party newspaper.

I was a confused young man but quickly realised that race or creed was not the problem.

I already had good friends who were multi-cultural and I knew in my heart that I had no right to target these people for any reason. I had much in common with these people, such as fashion and music, and had some memorable moments in my life with them which I look back upon fondly, and even as I now write, it brings a smile to my face.

I will go into more detail shortly.

For now, I had settled into a little bit of routine and had even managed to stay out of trouble for a while. I had a girlfriend who knew of my past but cared little about it and was certainly prepared to overlook it.

One of the local cinemas had decided to do a trial run with an all-night viewing of three films if I remember correctly. This was a novel idea which had been introduced successfully in other arears, and so the stage was set. The queues were long and it seemed likely it was going to be a profitable evening.

My girlfriend and I paid for our tickets, got a few treats and began to ascend the stairs leading to the foyer – oh dear.

At the top of the stairs stood my old adversary from Dewsbury Police, the infamous Donald Hurst and one of his colleagues who apparently wanted to simply check who was in attendance and who was not, and then he had the upper hand in any future interviews should anyone detained try using the cinema attendance in any future alibi.

Oh, he was certainly a wily old fox who was always one jump ahead.

His eyes lit up when he saw me and forced me up the wall with his hand about my throat. He seemed surprised that he had not seen me for a good period of time. My girlfriend informed him that maybe the reason was that I had turned over a new leaf.

His laughter echoed around the room and many of the other cinema-goers were staring over by now. Had I been alone I could quite easily have taken this situation in my stride but I was more than a little embarrassed for my girl.

I wrestled a little with him to ease the pressure of his hand on my throat but I could not break the hold completely. He gave me a few kicks to my shins and assured me that he would be coming for me at a later date, which I had no reason to doubt.

I doubt many police forces were any different to Dewsbury at this time. All of them with a constant flow of bullies who had no qualms about hitting you, even in a crowded cinema in front of many witnesses, because they really believed themselves to be above the law.

This bastard had taken a dislike to me many years before and by now I had also gathered there would be no romance here, even though I had blown him many kisses before, albeit from a safe distance.

I knew he would carry out his threat of coming for me.

He would make a point of stitching me up with any means at his disposal and I took the decision to make for pastures new and stay out of the firing line.

Goodbye Donald!!! All the best for your future career.

I will leave you in charge of your beloved Dewsbury but with my own safety in mind I will not be available for the foreseeable future.

Time for an adventure.

Huddersfield, here I come, and I am about to have one of the best periods of my life.

About time by my reckoning.

CHAPTER 10

I would soon settle into my new surroundings and the times I had been even the slightest bit racist tugged at my heart, because these people welcomed me with open arms and looked after me like I was one of their own. Huddersfield is another mill town, albeit with a very large Asian, Pakistani, and Afro-Caribbean community, and although only six miles from Dewsbury in distance it is like being on another planet to say it is that close.

I ended up squeezed into a tiny bedsit with six others on Wentworth Street up by the main park in the area, and days were filled with laughter. I won't ever forget a boy called Scooby whose bedsit it was, and had he chosen to, he could have refused entry to the rest of us when we showed up each night like waifs and strays. He lived there with his girlfriend but

I would often turn up with a half-caste girl called Pinky and another girl called Chelsea.

Bed space would be very limited and for this reason the floor would be our resting place, but it was preferable to sleeping rough on the street. Days would be spent shoplifting and evenings we would be frequenting the local West Indian Club on Venn Street, and afterwards maybe there would be a shabeen at Popsis Midway café by the railway viaduct.

It was at these shabeens I would meet many of the colourful characters I did, and this made me instantly fall in love with the area I had chosen to be my adopted home.

The police would always be aware of these illicit parties but for the sake of community relations would turn a blind eye. There was a resident band at the club called Jab Jab who even reached the dizzy heights of an appearance on Top of The Pops one time.

I would sometimes babysit a few of the children in the club while the band practised and for this duty I would be provided with regular meals and free entry to the club on a weekend when major bands would be playing.

Desmond Decker, The Pioneer, The Wailers Dave and Ansell Collins and all the top reggae bands, I would be able to watch all of them perform on a Saturday night and would be one of the few white people in attendance. Huddersfield was a big help to me in the difficult process of what I had to do, which was to grow up a little and stop being full of aggression.

It was not like that as soon as I arrived though,

because I would need funds and used Chelsea on a few occasions to provide me with the opportunity.

Could I say here and now I regret these events, but I was a different person at a different period in time. We would loiter about some of the local public houses until I would select a suitable victim who would be the worse for wear with the alcohol he had consumed. I would watch from a safe distance while Chelsea did all the flirting to get the victim into the spider's web with her charms, and lead him around the corner to a secluded spot with the promise of sex.

At the appropriate time and never so long that I would leave Chelsea in any sort of danger, I would make my appearance claiming to be the boyfriend, and punch the man forcibly to the ground and while the victim was disorientated, empty the contents of his pockets and vanish into the night with the proceeds.

It proved lucrative that first night as we both counted out bundles of screwed up notes typical of a drunken man putting change into his pockets from the many bars he had obviously visited. It wasn't actually a fortune but at least we would have no need to shoplift for the next few days.

I only committed this particular offence on one more occasion and even though it was not as profitable I think I had already decided I did not wish to commit street robberies.

My consciousness easily got the better of me and I never did it again.

The hours working at the club and being fed were sufficient for my daily needs and I would often have some Lebanese or Pakistani Black squeezed into my hand, and I would always be stoned with one resin or the other. These little treats I was given would make me a very laid back individual with no inclination to even clench a fist, let alone have a fight.

I was nurtured along by these people and I have a lot to thank them for.

It was not all sweetness and light because two local skinheads named Mick Folan and Spider had taken a little exception to me being in their area and also being as popular as I seemed to be, and I would feel a little bullied at times by this pair.

It didn't happen for too long though, because my friend Pecker had come over to stay in Huddersfield on my recommendation that it was a good area, and it would soon be game over for these two bullies as the town quickly became ours.

The world wasn't exactly our oyster but for the time being Huddersfield certainly was.

Pecker died in tragic circumstances a few years later. God bless his soul and rest in peace, my friend.

The last I heard of the two bullies was that they both got lengthy prison sentences for torturing some old man while they had him tied to a chair trying to get him to reveal where his money was.

No more than I would have ever expected from that pair and I hope they suffered every single day they were inside.

All of my memories of Huddersfield are good except for one or two incidents that do not bode well with me.

A friend of mine called Helen Rytka became one of Peter Sutcliffe's victims many years later, alongside the very same railway viaducts that I used to go partying at, and it's taken away all of the sparkle of that period.

Helen was the only victim that the repulsive Sutcliffe ever had sex with, and my heart bleeds for her and how she was left to die. I think of her often in that wood yard and how she met her end. Helen was a very beautiful girl and again, yet another victim of circumstances.

She would not have wished to be a prostitute when she was younger but unfortunately it ultimately led to her demise in a horrific way.

Shame on any of you who direct criticism at her or the many others who choose that option to earn money. None of you are without sin and have no right to cast stones.

Sutcliffe, may you burn in hell for your actions.

Other than the above I have many magical moments in that town and imagine it to be the exact same now, and very welcoming.

Because I was the new kid on the block I would be very popular with the local girls and had many sexual encounters, and never once did I look for a regular partner. I was young and I was having fun.

I had sex with my first coloured girl, something I would never imagine happening whilst my mind was being poisoned by my supposed friends in the National Front.

I had come a long way and I had no animosity

towards anyone.

As stated previously, the police seemed to leave the West Indian community well alone and that was perfect for me because I was right in the heart of it and I could get lost in the crowd.

I became good friends with a West Indian boy called Frankie, whose behaviour could be quite erratic but I had many hours of fun and laughter with him. He would speak in his native tongue quite often but very quickly, and I would simply smile when he did, presuming he had just informed me of the punchline.

We would both dress in our customary Harrington jackets and I soon realised I had many things in common with him; we would throw our arms around each other often and a strong bond would develop between us.

After a period of time when I left the area to return to Dewsbury, I would not see Frankie for many years and the very next time I saw him was on a landing at Armley prison in Leeds, and he was serving a five-year sentence for manslaughter.

He was not the same person as he struggled to come to terms with the fact that he had killed another man in a street fight.

The heavy medication he was taking was doing him no favours and gone was the bubbly character I had known; harsh as it may seem, I soon gave him a wide berth in the prison and would avoid him at all costs because he would talk in riddles and struggle to come to terms with what had happened.

There was no shortage of mad cap company in Huddersfield and one of the most bizarre, off-the-wall characters you could care to meet was a white boy called Fluff.

This lad would constantly be in his knee-high Doc Marten boots and was a very tall individual. He would go in too many of the town centre shops and point to items on a top shelf that would be out of reach of the assistants, and they would need to stand on whatever small steps to reach.

Meanwhile, we would be sat outside these shops wondering just what he was up to on this occasion.

At the very second any duped assistant would be distracted standing on the steps, Fluff would simply reach over and grab whatever was in reach and sprint from the shop.

Some of the funniest moments would be spent watching that lad running through a town centre with a full jar of sweets or packets of cigarettes tucked tightly under his arm while people chased him. His long legs and boots covered ground quicker than Usain Bolt – priceless memories. God bless all of you.

We were thieving little bastards but had many laughs with the antics we got up to.

I only ever got arrested once in all of my time spent in that area, so I was obviously doing something right for a change.

All good things come to an end and I had become a little homesick and returned to Dewsbury for a little catch up with my friends. I had already acquired quite a liking for cannabis but the times were changing fast now and many of my friends had become very laid back; a different era was evolving by way of fashion and also choice of drugs.

In the blink of an eye I was transformed from this sharp, snappy dresser in mod suits to an almost unrecognisable hippy of sorts clad in cheesecloth shirt, very scruffy jeans, and clogs on my feet.

This would be a very enlightening period for me as I experimented with LSD for long periods.

My friends and I were purchasing vast amounts of these little trips and the whole country was awash with them at that time.

I later discovered they had been mass produced at a little farmhouse in Wales which was raided by police in an early morning sting called Operation Julie.

Apparently the group had been infiltrated by an undercover police officer and he had managed to get in so deeply that he had even been shown the laboratory where it was produced. Once again reinforcing the old adage of never befriending strangers who are not part of your own circle.

It was calculated that once this factory was closed, street sales of LSD dropped dramatically by perhaps 80%, and from it being possible to purchase it quite cheaply, the price now went through the roof.

A funny anecdote I can recall is the few officers left at the farmhouse to contain the crime scene had not even appreciated that the presence of particles throughout the cottage was more than enough to have them hallucinating and stumbling about laughing whilst attempting to carry out their duties.

Now times were certainly hard and especially now our source of income had been taken away, but I would have found the money from somewhere and paid a king's ransom to watch those officers in that state.

I am willing to bet they enjoyed it that much they would have put in for extra shifts and overtime the following day.

But for now I would need to find other ways and means to earn money.

CHAPTER 11

I had become very slovenly in my appearance and always gave the look of being spaced out. I had grown my hair in long rats' tails in a rather large perm, and I would be taking any drug that was available. My preference would be LSD because of its unpredictable reaction. I had many pleasant trips leading to chaos, madness, and mayhem.

This drug will take you to many different levels and situations with its euphoric state, and obviously many may feel that it is not a drug they would feel comfortable experimenting with because of its potency. I would highly recommend everybody trying it at least once.

All that bullshit about finding your inner self and solving the mystery of the universe don't wash with me.

I wanted to take a trip and within half an hour be completely out of control and laughing uncontrollably; that was my only intention and to be quite honest I had my work cut out dealing with my outer self, let alone what lay hidden inside.

I was already a mixed-up character without adding more to the melting pot. My friend and close ally at the time was a Polish lad called Gabriel Chadonionek, or Chad for short, and we would trip on many occasions together. Aside from tripping, we would serve prison sentences together and also hitchhike around the country to various locations. We would be inseparable and I have his name tattooed prominently on the back of my hand. Nothing gay or anything, although many at the time thought we were a couple as we spent that much time together.

We would always find it amusing stood in the dock in courtrooms, laughing inwardly at how the magistrates or judge struggled to first pronounce my name, which can be quite difficult to master, and then Chad's surname. There would never even be one occasion when they would pronounce it correctly.

With the scarcity of LSD on the streets, boredom soon settled in and I hankered for more, and when the drug had been available earlier that year it had been arriving in bulk from St Ives in Cornwall. We decided that we should decamp to Cornwall, hoping that the source there would not have completely dried up.

My whole life has been spent on our motorways covering thousands of miles, and many drug dealers will tell you they do the same. If the merchandise is right and the price also, then any amount of distance will be covered to purchase drugs. Being in the drug trade is no different to being involved in any other business as deals are either done in retail or wholesale and often on credit.

Mention of travelling to St Ives would be on a weekly basis but had never been put into motion until a certain incident took place requiring me to get away from the area. I was meandering aimlessly around Dewsbury with a friend of mine, Ricky Sayer, and noticed on more than one occasion the presence of the same man following us nervously. Finally, he mustered the courage to actually speak by Dewsbury train station and asked if any of us lads had the correct time. I said, "Time we sorted out a little business," to which he replied, "Thank God for that, I haven't read the signs wrong. Does any of you lads suck?"

Perverted bastard, I thought as I said, "I do." After further exchanges I indicated that we should go somewhere a little less busy and the decision was taken to go to a disused dairy close at hand. Upon reaching the dairy he dropped his trousers in a state of arousal and stood proudly with his hands on his hips waiting for his reward for the five pounds that had been agreed. I bent down, giving the impression that I was about to do the deed, but instead brought my head up and butted him until he fell over with blood oozing from his mouth. He begged for mercy as I demanded his wallet.

He gave me the wallet and upon checking the contents, I discovered he only had fifteen pounds, which I took. I was not in a forgiving nature and gave him one last kick as I departed, and put down the house brick I intended to smash his face in with.

My violent tendencies would always be more than

excessive at this time and he may have been one of the luckier ones that I had let off lightly. I doubted he would go off to the police but rather than take the chance I gathered a few clothes together in a holdall bag and decided this was definitely the time to travel to Cornwall.

Chad and I were again soon at the start of our journey, and with our thumbs out by the M1 close to Wakefield. When the hitchhikers are two males it can sometimes take an eternity to get a lift because people are fearful of two strangers for obvious reasons. This journey was to be no different and whilst in the general area of the Midlands the decision was made to break up the journey by having a little stopover in Nuneaton.

This was the place I had traced my birth mother to a few years previously, and although the first contact had not gone too well we had still managed to maintain some form of contact, albeit randomly. I had a large extended family and many stepbrothers and sisters. I had to assure my stepfather that my days of trouble with any of the authorities were long over and we were making for Cornwall because we had employment waiting for us.

Formalities complete, I was welcomed with open arms and a bedroom was provided for our stay.

All of the younger siblings were excited at my presence and jumped all over me constantly.

I told my mother that me and Chad were going to have a look around the town and have a few beers. Chad liked the area and suggested we stay a little longer, and I knew he was dreading the long waits at the side of motorways waiting for lifts.

On the way up from the town we would need to pass the ground of the local rugby club and as if by telepathy we both began to look at each other and then the club. No words would be needed in these situations, bearing in mind the importance of remaining silent anyway. Easy access would soon be gained and some burglaries have additional bonuses to boost the rewards.

In this case it was the club house bar and while we forced our way into the gaming machines we would have the occasional drink from the bar. If I remember correctly we were having bottles of Babycham. Don't ask me to explain that one because I haven't got a clue, maybe we were feeling all "Christmassy". We certainly were singing carols once we emptied the machines, which were quite full.

After making our escape down the banks of the little brook close to the club, we high fived each other all the way back to my mother's home. After a little small talk, we decided on going up to the bedroom where we could share the proceeds out.

In the morning I indicated over the breakfast table that we may stay for a few more days and asked if it would be ok to do so. My stepfather said he had no problem with that as long as I stayed out of trouble in and around the town. *Bit late for that now*, I thought, but thought it wiser to keep that to myself.

I was already active and in a town where little was known of me; a free reign to pillage and plunder. I had never been one to waste an opportunity and this one was gilt-edged.

We would either be out on a night and burgling or looking for likely places while we were out during the day and returning on an evening at a later date.

I imagine all of the local burglars at that time would be getting questioned and arrested on a regular basis, and needing to proclaim their innocence.

We would be out and about and "on the mooch" almost every night of the week, and had a very busy workload. On one of these jaunts we had a little scare.

We were walking up Edward St., a road populated by immigrants, when a police car beckoned us over to ask where we had been and where we were now heading.

I leaned down to speak to the officer and whilst I did so, gently dropped my gloves wrapped around the screwdriver to the floor. While we completed formalities I pushed the implements of my trade under the car with my foot.

The joke amongst the officers seemed to be the length of Chad's surname, and the belief we were genuine, because nobody could make up a name up such as that. The usual request to search us was made and after finding nothing on us apologies were made and accepted and we were waved on our way and told to enjoy the rest of our night.

We remained composed until we were out of sight and then fell about laughing whilst throwing our arms about each other – phew, that was indeed a close call but it was a warning that additional patrols had been set up.

It was a warning that should have been taken on board and heeded, but as always in my life, I was a little too carefree for my own good.

We had been entering the local dairy and stealing large tins of ham during the night, even under the noses of the workforce. I say entering because there would be no need to burgle as the doors were of a plastic flap nature, giving the fork truck drivers easy access. We had been stealing whatever we could carry and selling it on at a reduced price on building sites the following day, but on this occasion we had been rather greedy and took a suitcase which we filled.

After leaving the premises our luck had run out as the police once again stopped us with the usual question/answer routine.

I claimed we had just hitchhiked into the area as a means of an explanation for the suitcase. Both the officers got out of the car and one requested to look inside the case – oh dear, the game is up.

The only good thing to come out of this arrest is I no longer had to carry the weighty case about.

There would be no bail because of my criminal background in Yorkshire and the same applied to Chad. I tried to give the magistrate an absurd explanation that as in France there were crimes of passion, so at times there should be crimes of hunger.

I could have perhaps made a case out of it had I only the one tin in my possession, but twenty-five tins was maybe a little too excessive. The magistrate smiled as he remanded me into custody, where my hunger would be accommodated by three meals a day in Her Majesty's Prison, Winson Green in Birmingham.

Did I have any need for concern? Would it be like Yorkshire prisons?

Not one bit of difference to be honest.

Lots of hustle and bustle, lots of obese warders, lots of shouting, and last but by no means least, lots of attitude. They hadn't met me before and I had lots of attitude myself – hello Winson Green.

CHAPTER 12

Anyone who thinks being a criminal is a glamorous lifestyle need only enter one of these institutions for a few weeks to realise it is far from glamorous. Winson Green would be no different, albeit being much bigger than my usual place of residence in Leeds.

Obviously the bigger the prison, the bigger the percentage of bizarre characters who are in there. A curious couple in there while I was on remand were the Littlejohn brothers, who were category A prisoners and guarded around the clock due to their recent escape from Mountjoy Prison in Ireland.

This pair had been robbing banks at gunpoint in Ireland with the supposed intention of infiltrating the IRA. When one robbery went wrong and they ended up in custody in mitigation, they claimed they were working for British Intelligence at the time and the robberies were simply to convince the IRA they were genuine criminals and were to be trusted.

Now the matter becomes complex because the British authorities denied all knowledge of the men or their activities. Because they had made their claims in an open court their lives were now at risk from Republican prisoners.

For some strange reason they were both placed in protective custody at all times and under constant supervision. Despite these constant observations both of the brothers supposedly escaped from this maximum security prison, and not only escaped the prison but even managed to get all the way back to England without being discovered.

Unsurprisingly, in my opinion, they were recaptured within days of reaching England and ensconced in Winson Green while a decision was reached on their futures. They would be kept apart from the regular prisoners and could often be seen exercising with just each other for company.

All a little mysterious and yet another example of British Intelligence, and in particular MI5, at their most devious.

The escape from Mountjoy still leaves many unexplained answers, and the warders on duty that night have little or nothing to say on the matter. This all took place in the early to mid-1970s and they both seemed to be well protected whilst they were in Winson Green.

The whole prison would be alive with conversations to do with the Littlejohns, who had gained celebrity status amongst the other inmates.

I presumed they would have many secret meetings with special branch while they languished in their prison cells, but I doubted they ate the same prison diet as the rest of the inmates. It was all a very strange situation but in a prison anything that breaks the mundane routine and creates excitement is a welcome distraction.

We would be stoned on cannabis most days, or maybe the odd cup of hooch, the homemade alcoholic drink that could be purchased if you knew the right person to see. There would never be enough work to go round and employ everyone and the majority of us would be spending 23 hours a day in our cells, only being let out for the customary one hour's exercise a day.

If that sounds glamorous to any of you then be my guest and go and have a little stay.

It is far from the "holiday camp" image that the media would lead you to believe. My only consolation was that I had been locked up for a monetary value rather than the usual instances of violence.

I had long since promised myself that should I go behind a prison door again it would be for a profit margin as opposed to senseless violence – it mattered little though, what the offence was.

The fact remained I was stuck in yet another shithole of a prison and I needed to put my brain in gear and find a satisfactory way out of there. I wrote letters in mitigation to the magistrates and prepared my defence in advance.

Very rarely would I use a solicitor because I always

felt more than capable of representing myself, and I always used to feel that if at any time I could present myself as being a little articulate, it could sway proceedings in my favour.

Ever the optimist.

I sort of enjoyed Winson Green because it was so vast it was possible to get lost in the crowd and melt into the background.

Because I had a pending court case, the last thing I would need was any incidents, and while on remand it is always important to keep one's head down, thereby creating a favourable report for court indicating I had been no trouble and practically a model prisoner. It's a means to an end and we all play the system to our advantage, especially if one is on remand and still has a slight possibility of actually walking free.

A strange incident took place while we were on remand.

A friend of ours who had been drinking with us on regular occasions in Nuneaton had begun to miss us and our antics, and took the decision to join us in the prison.

Tommy Phillips was a local character in Nuneaton and well known to the locals. He is dead now, God bless his soul. Tommy, after getting drunk, decided to cause a fight and the altercations ended with him stabbing a random stranger and because of the serious nature of the crime, he found himself immediately remanded to the same prison as me and Chad.

Tommy got his wish and was very excited to have his reunion on the exercise yard or the few occasions we were let out for meals. The twist in the tale is that eventually Tommy received two and a half years' imprisonment for the assault, while Chad and me were given a term of some novel punishment introduced that very day we went to court.

It is now commonplace everywhere in the sentencing system, but at that time was completely new.

We were in actual fact the first two to be sentenced to Community Service on the proviso we resided at a sort of halfway house called McIntyre House on Edward Street, Nuneaton – who cared what it was?

We had just been on remand for five weeks and I had never before walked away free from a courtroom. Did he really say "you are free to go"? Did he say that?

I wrote to Tommy throughout his sentence to give him what comfort I could, but I imagined he felt very foolish indeed getting a substantial sentence for the sake of a few weeks with us and then us walking free. He would have been shocked to say the least.

But not as shocked as me.

Hoorah, we were out, but what the fuck was Community Service? What was all that about?

Once the dust had settled the probation officer explained in detail what was required of us both, and that would be a minimum of fifteen hours' unpaid work per week irrespective of us having a full-time paid job or not.

Our immediate problem was the press were practically camped outside of McIntyre House and wanted photographs of criminals working in the community, and so made it difficult to even get the hours worked. We had been given the maximum sentence of 240 hours which was rather excessive but I didn't really care. It was better than a prison cell.

A more immediate problem was that Chad and I were out and back in our usual routine of drug-induced states or an excess of alcohol; we were becoming very bored of this scenario and the restrictions the halfway house imposed upon us, so we took the decision to make for pastures new.

Back to Yorkshire would be the choice.

My mother and stepfather had been disappointed with my term in prison after I had assured them I was a reformed character, and they no longer spoke to me.

Homeward bound seemed the easy option and we told no one and had no goodbyes to say.

We jumped on a train and set off, of course without tickets.

Obviously we did not want to be in breach of the first bit of leniency I had ever received so at the first opportunity presented ourselves at the probation services in Dewsbury with a request to transfer the sentence to Yorkshire.

It could not be denied really, and after due deliberation with all of the parties concerned, the sentence was exchanged.

No such problem here with the media because it had already been a standard sentence for a while and the novelty had worn off, I suppose. So we got our opportunity to get some of our hours worked off.

I attended some places and met nice people who would write more hours in the attendance book than

I had actually worked. This gave me the chance to lower my hours much quicker, which was useful because by now I had a regular job in a rag warehouse as well, and I would be constantly tired with the 40 hours in my regular job and the 15 hours Community Service.

A funny occasion was when I was sent to the Blind Centre where the scaffold had already been erected for me and another lad to paint the ceiling. Every now and again one of the blind people would come into the room with the white stick, checking and feeling for the scaffold.

They would ask as to how it was coming on and I would assure them it was looking good although in reality I had done little or no work. The lid being off the paint tin would be enough to suggest that some work had been done, given the blind person's sense of smell.

Eventually the room would be complete but if I was ever given the chance to swing the lead a little or grab an hour's sleep, then I would do just that. This was unpaid work, remember, and no way was I there to sweat blood.

Things came to a head one day when I was sent to an Oxfam Centre to do some unpaid work. I was just sat waiting to hear my duties and having a cigarette and reading my paper. Out of the blue a voice boomed, "You can put that fucking newspaper down, you're not here to read."

Oh dear. I thought. *Here's one of them who thinks I should be in prison and Community Service shouldn't even be in existence.*

I bit my lip for a while and he told me to sweep the big yard. I did as I was told and when he returned I thought I'd done a good job, but he was not happy and informed me I had missed an area and wanted me to move 200 paving slabs from one spot to another and then sweep underneath.

Needless to say I grabbed him by the throat and asked him if he wanted to end up under the paving slabs.

His earlier bravado soon left him as he scampered away.

I left the site and informed the probation office I wasn't prepared to do any work again. She sympathised with me and tried to make me reconsider, but my mind was made up because no way could I place myself alongside a man of that calibre because I would not be responsible for my actions.

I was placed in breach and put before the magistrates, but in my favour I had completed 107 hours and the magistrate decided that the original sentence of 240 hours was very excessive because the average sentence in Yorkshire since the introduction had been 120 hours; they felt I had paid my dues anyway and instead waived the remainder and replaced it with a six-month probation term.

Result! Don't know what I was doing right but I was pleasing someone looking down on me.

To the gentleman with the yard brush and the flagstones, may I say to you that someone must have also been looking down on you that day. You were a very lucky man indeed – we both had a result.

I was clear of everything and just had to listen to

get another boring probation officer for the next six months.

Would I handle that? You bet your life I could.

Goodbye Community Service.

CHAPTER 13

I had always had someone who was deemed responsible for me. Probation or Parole Officers, Psychiatrists, Social or Case Workers, you name it and I have sampled them all. Not that it made a blind bit of difference because I had great difficulty coming to terms with and conforming to my authoritative body.

Occasionally I would have all the best intentions and would leave the company of one of the above with good thoughts, or being positive one day, but a crisis could develop very quickly within the next day or so. I was diagnosed with depression at a very early age and I still get treated for it to this day.

I have always seemed to be on one medication or another and I don't doubt that everyone who was responsible for me in a medical capacity had my best interests at heart, but the bottom line was they did not have to live my life and so could not possibly ever fully understand the complicated lifestyle I led.

Yes, I suppose illicit drugs took a big toll on me, but when you have nothing or no one in life then it becomes quite easy to rely on alternative crutches to ease the burden. None of this is self-pity. The paths I chose in life were my own and so repercussions from my choices would have to be accepted.

During my life I would have lots of long periods in employment and in actual fact I have a total in excess of thirty years in gainful employment, so I did try to toe the line and do what was expected of me. Having said that, I have never once had a job since I left school when I have not needed to work overtime to supplement my wages. No employer ever seems to pay an adequate wage and so it becomes easier to resort to crime in times of hardship.

The retail industry is no different to any other workplace and the only difference in any of them is that many of the white collar workers on a more substantial wage feel no need to be apart from their families on weekend. While I was a manual worker and management did not feel a need to be supervising, then I would take the opportunity to either play cards or sleep. In a retail setting, if they chose to leave the younger members of staff in charge then I along with many other shoplifters, would take full advantage of that and simply walk out of any store with very expensive items.

This was the way of my world and often during the periods I had a job, I would use that as an opening to sell drugs on the shop floor or fake perfumes and aftershave. I seemed to be always involved in one criminal activity or another on a daily basis. None of it seemed wrong to me and just seemed to be the way of the world.

Having a job is the mainstay of most people but for me it was being occupied and away from the crime culture. Selling things on the shop floor did not really qualify for what I deemed to be criminal activity. To me that was simply a side-line but unfortunately I had one shop floor manager who had taken a dislike to me, and thought he would create a few problems and bring about a dismissal.

Why bother being amongst these people? I would think, and I hurled a load of abuse at this manager as I emptied my locker, but at least the police had not been called for. *Why bother even trying to go straight? Fuck this. Point me in the direction of an earner.*

I'd had more than enough of clocking in and out and being accountable to people.

The term "rat race" is a perfect description and no way was I intending to be part of it.

I was bored in a factory setting anyway and wanted that little bit of extra excitement to get my adrenalin rush.

First port of call after leaving the factory was one of the local public houses to raise my spirits and get me in the mood for devilment.

I had been told of a recent scam that had been "worked" up and down the country with a great deal of success, and decided to attempt it myself. I would need to write a letter to my local bank and await the reply with the bank's heading at the top of the letter. I would now need a girlfriend of mine to transpose a typed up letter, albeit incorporating the bank's heading on it, thus giving official endorsement to what the bank "supposedly" intended the customer to do.

Once the bank closed for the day the letter would be placed on the night deposit box implying that due to unforeseen circumstances the security box would be inaccessible for one night only, but extra security had been employed and to feel free to deposit the package through the bank's letterbox with details of the customer.

Bank letterboxes are very deep and my friend and I had already placed a lot of screwed up newspapers into the letterbox until it had reached the stage where I could put my hand through and make contact with the top.

We loitered about a street corner and observed from a safe distance, and witnessed one or two read the "official" letter but disregard the instructions as to what to do. We were giving up any hope of this becoming fruitful when one of the market traders in his uniform seemed to believe the letter to be genuine, and wandered over to the bank's letterbox and deposited a large hessian wallet with that day's invoices.

We watched in amazement and could not believe our luck, but if anything we ruined it through our haste. Once the man had departed we raced across to the bank and I fumbled about until I came into contact with the parcel and pulled it out.

A passer-by shouted inquisitively as to what we were doing and we just had to make our escape quickly. Just our luck as well to have chosen one of the smaller traders who had only placed a few hundred pounds in, rather than the thousands of pounds we had anticipated and dreamt of all throughout the previous week when we hatched the plan.

But even so, it had worked and it amazed me how gullible people could be.

Had "Butch and Sundance" not shown me just how easy it was to take people in and dupe them?

I felt a little guilty that it was a regular working man who had lost his day's takings, as I would much rather it had been one of the bigger department stores' takings. Maybe we should have waited a while longer for more deposits but what if there had not been any more? What if a patrolling policeman had stumbled upon the letter?

We got excited in the moment and who cared that we were hasty?

We had beer tokens, and after an equal share out and the burning of the invoices and wallet, we made for the pub.

I was staggered how easy it was considering I had only heard of this scam a few weeks before. I swore my friend to secrecy and told him I knew another little earner that needed two of us working as a team, but we would need to wait for a busy weekend in the town and it would only work in the bigger pubs that had two bars working, albeit with one till.

I should probably have spent my time better and sought another job but I suppose I was in one of my "fuck it" periods.

I preferred easy pickings and if they were there to be had then I would find a way.

That coming weekend it was time to put my next "sting" to the test while we still had a few notes around us which we needed to pull it off. We would both go into a pub but order drinks in different rooms. The notes I had in my pocket, I would have previously stained with dye. I would give one of these twenty pound notes to my friend and he would get served in the other bar.

Once I noticed he had been served I would also purchase a drink with a five pound note.

Upon receiving my change, I would question the amount of change and insist I had given a twenty pound note. Occasionally an argument would ensue but I would state that I had only been paid that day, and would display my pay packet which obviously was full of the stained twenties, and request that the till be checked. At the top of the pile would be the stained twenty.

Some would apologise and immediately give you the balance, but some would say to come back at the end of evening when the float could be checked. That would be a case of not returning. This could not be done at many pubs and it certainly didn't make a small fortune, but what it did was go towards a free night out.

It's not always the size of the reward, it's the actual completion of a task we had set out to do and our next pints would be consumed with raucous laughter. It all becomes a game of wits and I have no shame in anything I did during these times.

Yes, I was a chancer, but we are surrounded by con men and shysters who are bankers and politicians, or traders on our stock markets who syphon millions off with their corrupt ways of life.

Who on earth would want to look down their noses at me in comparison to these sort of people? But unfortunately some do.

I really don't care, if I'm honest, I am simply detailing my life and the style in which I had to live it to survive. If anything, at this particular period in time I am serving out my apprenticeship.

In later chapters my life of crime takes a serious turn for the worse with the introduction of firearms and very major illegalities. For now, I was still reasonably young and was just getting by the best I could and having lots of fun while I did so. I was not a house burglar and I tried never to take from people who had less than me or were in a similar situation.

I readily agree with our older generation who claimed they could leave their doors open without fear of thefts or burglaries, but in reality nobody had anything of value to steal. I stated in the earlier chapters it can all be blamed on the consumer society we have created and everyone wanting everything and wanting it now.

Of course everyone could leave their doors open back in time, because there would be nothing worth stealing.

Nowadays it takes teams of two and three burglars to carry the booty away, there is that much of it.

I have never burgled anyone's house and nor will I ever do so.

I like to think I still have morals and standards but I will let all of you who read this be the judge of that.

CHAPTER 14

Unemployment was rife up north at this time, and mainly because of the closure of the steelworks and pits. I had been a shop steward in the steel industry for many years and after Ian McGregor had been drafted in from America by Margaret Thatcher (how I hate that bitch) to decimate firstly the steel industry and then the coal mines, times became very hard.

The northern people are renowned for their community spirit and this period would be no different.

I would receive strike pay, albeit a very meagre sum, and I would need to attend Bradford Town Hall to get food parcels or visit soup kitchens at times for the occasional hot meal. Crime statistics at this time must have gone through the roof and even friends of mine who had been upstanding figures in the community their whole lives turned to crime to put food on the table. Most of it would be petty offences but some, out of sheer desperation, went a little too far and committed armed robbery.

Fortunately for me, I resisted the temptation to go on one such robbery at a local petrol station with two of my friends. It was a disaster from start to finish and although the "gun" was a cheap imitation, it matters little because the intent is there.

It taught me never to become involved in these sort of robberies which seemed to be the crime of choice at either building societies, garages, or corner shops. The rewards would be small and in the main a few hundred pounds, which is less than a week's wage, rather than the thousands hoped for.

There were the times when chutes had been introduced into many of these small businesses and once a reasonable amount of money had been taken in trade, then the money would be sent down the said chute, therefore ensuring no great amount of money could be stolen.

I hadn't appreciated before just how stern the sentencing tariff was for this particular crime but anyone caught participating could expect a minimum of five years' imprisonment. I discovered this when I was at Wakefield Crown Court and watched my friends receive six and seven years respectively, and the sum of money involved amounted to no more than 187 pounds.

Had I chosen to go with them on that fateful evening I would have been serving a similar sentence for an equal share of perhaps 50 pounds.

I promised myself faithfully to never at any time even consider getting involved in anything that drastic.

Since then I have witnessed first-hand in many prisons young lads from all over the country serving long sentences, and some of them were not even armed when they committed the robberies, instead having cucumbers or other objects giving the impression they were actually armed.

The fear factor would still exist, I suppose, with the victims, and for all the sentences seem long they also may be justified. I am so glad I declined to be an armed robber.

Instead I chose to become involved in drugs yet again, because the rewards can be astronomical given the right set of circumstances and clientele. Obviously the circle of friends need to be small and very much trusted.

Drugs became a part of my life for many years and I did not see it as such a big deal... if you pardon the pun. It was not like I touted for business outside school playgrounds or targeted a younger market.

I sold my wares to consenting adults and our choices should be of our own making.

Yes, it's illegal, but I have never felt a need to be answerable to anyone as far as this matter is concerned.

My choices in life are exactly that! This was now big boy business and I found myself in some very dangerous situations. This form of "employment" would not be everyone's cup of tea and there would be no union representative or health and safety issues should anything go wrong, as it did on many occasions.

More hours could be spent on this job than any regular employment, and days at a time could be spent on one or another motorway; my partner at that time could expect to see me every two to three days and only then if I was passing on a motorway close to home, and even then it would only be a fleeting visit to perhaps offload some money.

My friend and I could be in Liverpool one minute and then London the next, or many other calling points we would use.

For obvious reasons I prefer not naming particular people or places for fear these individuals are still doing a little work and using trusted routes. With the introduction of vehicle identification cameras, it has now become difficult to do the things that we did then, although I am sure it will never prevent it fully.

On one particular business trip we had been driving long distances for perhaps two days and had hardly slept at all due to consuming large amounts of amphetamine sulphate to increase our awareness and energy levels.

Lack of sleep and energy can increase anxiety and paranoia levels but we had a deadline to meet and so continued on our journey to complete our business for an increased order to some customers in Middlesbrough. The problem now was that we were picking up the amount of amphetamine from one source to drop straight to another, and because of our already drug-induced state, we had no means of determining the quality of the drugs we had picked up.

We carried on from Leeds to the public house car park in Middlesbrough and all of the usual procedure was taking place with no complications, when suddenly another man jumped into the back of the car and placed a gun to my head. "I hope you lads are in no rush to nowhere," he demanded.

This was no imitation gun and the situation became very much more alarming when he told my friend to drive and he would instruct him when to stop, which turned out to be a very shabby-looking council estate.

He said he had no intention of robbing us, to ease our fears. His concerns were that he had been placing his orders with us for a long time but because this was a much bigger order he needed to protect his interests and ensure the goods were of a good standard before he was prepared to part with his money.

This would involve one of the residents of the neighbourhood placing some of the powder onto a spoon and cooking the contents up, after a little dilution with water and a filter tip within the spoon to absorb any impurities to prepare for injection.

I find this practice absolutely disgusting but on this one occasion I wanted everything to be above board and acceptable as he tied a shoelace tightly round his arm. It seemed an eternity before the recipient gave a thumbs up in approval and everyone breathed a sigh of relief, especially my friend and I.

In moments like that it is most definitely a case of being in the shooting line (no pun intended).

All of us shook hands and completed the

formalities of exchanging the product and the money.

It was a serious lesson that times were beginning to change quite quickly, and firearms certainly became a little bit more prominent than they had previously been. Yes, I had become a little fearful for my safety and I will explain in later chapters just how widespread and commonplace guns had become.

All the way back to Leeds, my friend and I discussed what had just taken place and perhaps the need to arm ourselves in case of any future situations that could ever lead to us being robbed.

At this point I would like to make it clear that I neither admit nor deny at any time being armed or coming into contact with firearms. I would not be prepared to admit that I had, or perhaps I would if you put a loaded gun to my head, ha ha.

I make light of the matter now but situations like the one I described certainly make the hairs on your neck stand on end. Does anyone still think it's a glamorous lifestyle?

Would you want to earn your money in this manner?

We would meet with seasoned criminals one minute and then at the other end of the scale we would do business with some of the new age travellers around the country for large amounts of LSD.

Some of these people would not only be very colourful but also be very articulate and educated. All the derogative terms labelling them "crusty" or some other insult are in my opinion uncalled for. They are simply people attempting to create an alternative lifestyle, and who are we to deny them that?

I have sat around campfires with some of them, but would readily admit I refused the offer of food from the cauldron by the fire. I would be concerned with the contents, perhaps falsely believing it to be full of hedgehogs or other creatures. I had no objection to their choice of lifestyle but it would not be something I would wish to enter into.

My friend and I would conduct business and purchase thousands of trips of LSD from them, and business would always be conducted pleasantly and with no cause for concern.

I did not doubt that they also had firearms on site should they need to call upon them.

On one of these occasions when we went to purchase them, my friend counted sheet after sheet to ensure we had the correct amount.

This was on some British Aerospace land in Bristol where the travellers were camped, and after we had completed the business and left the site strange things started to happen.

We hit the motorway and headed back to our home town but my friend seemed to be giggling initially, but then laughing uncontrollably. It soon transpired that his fingers had become soaked whilst counting the trips and each time he had a cigarette the LSD would be consumed via his lips.

I could not drive to relieve him but it soon became apparent the journey would need to be completed at a later stage. Numerous cars would be beeping their horns as our speed decreased to perhaps twenty miles per hour, and the importance of reaching somewhere safe was crucial.

We finally came to a halt at some motorway services close to Weston Super Mare and my friend practically fell out of the car laughing hysterically. We knew we would need to stay here for a reasonably long period of time and I would soon tire of babysitting my friend, so rather than do that I took the decision to consume a trip myself.

In for a penny, in for a pound.

I would be playing catch up but within half an hour I would also be giggling and laughing uncontrollably.

If anyone can ever recall coming across two people such as us that night behaving like complete lunatics, then my friend and I were the culprits.

I don't think I have ever laughed as long and hard at everyone and everything.

A word of warning!

When buying trips of LSD from travellers then proceed with caution because they will be very freshly manufactured and of a very strong nature – but what a night.

CHAPTER 15

On one of our excursions to Brixton in London to do yet another deal, but this time for a large amount of cannabis resin, we would find ourselves caught up in a turf war going off between rival gangs, and we would be thankful for getting out of the area safely.

We had been taught a serious lesson in Middlesbrough that we should both never be together at the same time whilst carrying a large amount of money. Upon arrival in London we booked into a Holiday Inn close to the West End because we planned on having a little fun whilst we were in the capital.

At the initial meeting we were under the impression we were dealing with the major players of that area and we were unaware of all the recent disputes with these rival gangs. Whilst we discussed weights and measures and amounts of money we heard an almighty bang from a van parked close to the public house we were meeting at.

On further inspection we realised the van belonging to our suppliers had been fire bombed in broad daylight by way of a warning, and I was glad we had left the money in a safe place. I talked my friend into postponing our business until a later date, knowing full well I had no inclination to ever even frequent this area again, let alone the pub we were in.

There had to be easier ways to earn a living, surely.

In my opinion I was still in my formative years but overnight I had become an adult in what was very much a twilight world. Don't get me wrong, the rewards were more than satisfactory, but the situations were becoming fraught with danger.

By now I had a partner and a child to consider and would never inform her of any life-threatening encounters I had been involved in for fear of scaring her.

It was not a decision I took lightly but I decided to put myself on the back burner for a while and take myself out of the present situation. I needed a little relaxation and maybe a family holiday to recharge my batteries.

I promised my friend I would return to "the game" at the earliest opportunity, which he believed to be weeks, but I knew it would instead be months.

I felt much better in myself and even managed to gain a little weight, as when I was constantly on the road and taking appetite suppressants, without realising, I had become a little gaunt and underweight.

I was sleeping much better and quite content with my life, and the choice of when to return to "the game" was taken out of my hands with the sad news that my friend had been arrested in a live situation and had been remanded into custody with the likelihood of a steep sentence.

I would need an alternative source of income for the time being because the funds from my semi-retirement fund had almost ran dry.

I had liked the quiet life I had been living and would have preferred to continue living that way, but unfortunately it was virtually impossible to acquire full time employment so I would need to resort to crime yet again.

I had been told a way and means of breaking into the cash boxes in public phone boxes. This would entail standing some firm object beneath the box and then with a hand, jack pumping and pumping until firm contact is made. At this given moment it is necessary to try and stand back as far as possible because when the pressure gets too much it will shatter in all directions and the fragmented pieces could cause serious injury.

This may not seem a rewarding way to commit crime but many hundreds of pounds can be found in each box.

An early indication that the box was full was when the phone indicates it is only available for emergency calls. In effect, it is telling you no more coins can be accepted and basically giving one the green light that it is in need of emptying.

Ordinance survey maps would be purchased and a

note would be made as to which areas and phones had been previously visited. It would be possible to earn in excess of a thousand pounds by simply emptying a few boxes per evening.

Caution would be needed when cashing in the loose change, especially the smaller value coins. An earner is an earner whichever way you look at it, and if it is possible to earn more in one night than you could in a week's gainful employment, then only a fool would refuse.

Whether I liked it or not I was a criminal in every sense of the word and nothing I seemed to do was legitimate any more. I would never show remorse or have regrets for what I did because my reality and my world was that I had a mortgage to pay and a family to feed and I cared little where the money came from.

By now I was toughened to the ways of the world and just treated everything matter-of-factly. Needs must, and I was the head of the household and needed to provide.

I make no excuses for that, although in my defence a little I would tell you that up the north at that time most of the industries had long since been decimated and held no future for many of us. A bigger problem for me was that I actually enjoyed what I did.

I thrived on living on the edge, and after terms of forced or unforced absences I would soon wish to return to the fray.

Illicit drugs would always be my career choice with regard to the profit margins involved, and I had recently met some army squaddies based in Germany.

NEVER A DULL MOMENT

When some of them were on leave at weekends they would take the opportunity to travel across the border to Holland. When they returned any searches at the border would be minimal and in many cases non-existent. They would simply need to flash their army ID and be waved through with the mountains of alcohol for their colleagues in the barracks.

In amongst these cans would be the occasional can which although giving the appearance of a regular can, would have actually have been modified inside to have half of the actual liquid content, and the other half would contain high quality cocaine.

Unfortunately, the world we live in, everyone has a price and is capable of being corrupted and the drugs would be able to reach the UK. Again, I would not be prepared to detail the routes that made it possible.

At this time, I met a particular soldier I disliked because of his attitude and thought perhaps he was taking a little more cocaine than he should have been. He was far too confident and cocksure of himself as he boasted of his exploits.

I decided to cease doing business with him when he bragged of one of these exploits and showed me a photograph of the married woman he was sleeping with. It turned out the lady in question was the wife of one of the SAS soldiers under arrest in Gibraltar for the shooting of IRA suspects in a supposedly "shoot to kill" policy.

They were not allowed to leave the island until the case had been heard and reached its conclusion. Was this soldier mental?

No way did I wish the timing to be wrong for me

and to be caught in this man's company when he got his come tuppences, which I felt he surely would. So I took the decision to go absent without leave. I've always been a brave man, but not that brave. I made myself scarce at the earliest chance.

Incidentally, all of the SAS soldiers were found not guilty and allowed to leave the island.

If the soldier I speak of did get any repercussions for his actions I would say they were deserved.

It would be possible to purchase firearms from many of our military, and it did not need to come from their own arsenal. Many of them would have been brought back from the constant war zones they visited during their tours of duty, and some would supplement their wages with the sale of these guns. Many would be antiquated but if in working order would be purchased nevertheless.

Some of you may find that alarming until you consider a lot of our soldiers are working-class boys from poverty-ridden communities. They are certainly not blessed with adequate incomes while serving in our armed forces and an alternative source of income is very tempting to some.

They are not difficult to find and in most cases some of them lived on our own estates and could simply be approached while on leave and having a pint in their local pub. Some could be friends and some could also be drug users themselves, which would make the task of approaching them easier.

I should imagine it still takes place to this day. Perhaps even more so considering how shabbily our soldiers are protected while deployed to these far off conflicts.

I salute every one of you but I reserve a special salute for all the soldiers who brought our supplies over from Holland.

It was about this time that the drug squad in Yorkshire began to take a special interest in me, far too much attention for my liking.

A friend of mine who used to drive me about on his scooter making deliveries had been arrested for some minor offence, and I accompanied his girlfriend to the police station to see how much longer he would be detained.

On arrival at the police station I observed two plain clothes officers having a good search in my friend's helmet, and in particular the lining. He had been arrested by uniformed officers, so who were these two and what were they searching for? Instant alarm bells.

Obviously drug squad.

I made my exit and also told my friend's girlfriend to go and clear her house of anything incriminating as quickly as she could in case they showed up with a warrant.

Nothing came of that night but it had put me on my guard and I would never carry anything about my person for the time being. I would often take a shortcut via a disused railway line to reach the town centre and as I did so, I was approached by two men who claimed to be railway police and said due to the many thefts on the railway lately, would it be possible to search me?

In a situation like this, any undercover police only get one opportunity to show their hand and so need it to be a success or their cover is blown. I smiled and smirked while they did a search that revealed nothing and asked them if that concluded matters, could I now go about my business and on my way?

They did not like my manner at all and one of them shouted that I was committing a crime by trespassing on the railway. I retreated and after taking to the road, shouted, "Thank you officer, my shoes will remain cleaner going this route."

"You cocky bastard!" he shouted to me, to which I replied, "Yes, there seems to be a few of us about today."

I knew they wouldn't go away easily and my days were numbered.

I had recently split with my partner and saw no reason to remain in the area and put myself on offer.

After sorting out arrangements for contact with my son, I left the area and put myself a safe distance from my predators.

CHAPTER 16

It was no great inconvenience to me because many of my contacts were situated in other areas of the country. St Albans, Hemel Hemsted, Bedford, Derby, Wakefield, and other towns or cities.

I would serve up customers in all of these places and meet at train station, bus terminals, or even the odd race track now and again if we fancied betting a few horses and mixing business with pleasure.

With a lot of my main contacts I would memorise their phone numbers or have a certain code worked out to identify who was who to protect their identity, although preference would be to use different public phone boxes on each occasion. It is always better to be safe than sorry because should things go wrong, lengthy prison sentences can be expected, but having said that, the safety concern can reach epic proportions of paranoia and especially if any of us were regular users as well.

Most of us would be users and we had all the best intentions of keeping our heads clear and focussed for any proposed business deals, but the drawback was that if any of us had been partying throughout the weekend, the need for a tiny livener to wake oneself up would be the order of the day.

One line would soon lead to another.

Most business deals would be done in the early part of the week on what we called "dead days".

The problem would be that consumption on a weekend regarded as acceptable would always stretch into the week; the cycle becomes a continuous one and being reliant on the drug soon becomes a way of life. All of us believe we can control everything and we do not have a problem.

I was no different and always felt I had done well throughout my life because although I had taken practically every drug in existence, I had never woken up craving anything. Or so I thought.

I had recently been introduced to crack cocaine and found it so enjoyable that I did not appreciate just how reliant I had become on those little rocks. I would constantly have the one ash tray set aside to keep clean ash in to use in the process of lighting a crack pipe up. Some people with time on their hands would produce some magnificent pipes like pieces of art.

I would marvel at some of these works of art and even purchased one myself. My kitchen would often see me mixing bicarb soda with cocaine until it was solidified and ready to inhale. My problems began when I started to use while I was on business journeys, and therefore put the situation at risk.

I was a recipe for disaster, although I would not admit that myself.

Obviously I would never carry a pipe around while up and down the motorways because should the driver and I be pulled over, the pipe itself would have been a clear signal we were involved in drug use and that could result in the car having a search.

It would be very easy to improvise and buy a small can of Red Bull and empty the contents, and then pierce a few holes in the area that has been sank in the can. Place clean ash in the indentation with a tiny rock and then light and inhale the fumes in the hole meant for drinking the Red Bull.

My driver would refuse because he preferred being focussed and in control while he was driving, although he admitted at a later date that he was concerned about how much I was using.

The can would be thrown away but I would be buying another can on near enough every occasion we were stopping.

I began to miss appointments and deadlines or forgot important numbers, and the whole previously established business began to fall like a house of cards. Word quickly spread that I had spiralled out of control and could not be trusted to conduct any business as it should be done.

My health began to suffer and I became a very psychotic individual. I volunteered readily for therapy as I realised this situation could not continue. Psychiatrists always piss me off though, because they always search for a jigsaw piece that is unobtainable really. Analysis after analysis follows and over the years it would be no exaggeration to say I have had about ten different ones.

Some blame my ecstasy period, or one will blame the LSD and damage to my brain cells. I was even once knocked out cold by a spanner and one half of my head is completely numb and has no nerves — even this has been blamed for my mental issues.

Here is my firm opinion.

Why don't we all just accept that it's simply the lifestyle I lead, and with or without drug abuse my mind would still be disturbed. I was disturbed as a child long before I consumed drugs so instead of preferring all of these textbook opinions, why don't we just accept that the jigsaw will never be completed? I will always have a piece missing but for now I needed patching up and to be given a little to put me back on track; the option of being locked and secured in a mental facility seemed the best option to cleanse myself of this drug.

It was no big deal to me, I had been in mental institutions before and it held no fears.

During my life I spent eleven years in prison or mental asylums and I do not mention much of them because there is little to tell. It's a boring, mundane spell in any prison.

I have told stories in my previous book of prison life but the usual routine is that every day you say, "Yes sir," or, "No sir," and you are back out on the street in next to no time.

Or you say, "Fuck off, you cunt," to just about

every warden and have shitloads of attitude and spells in solitary, and spend more time in prison for bad behaviour. I preferred the latter.

But an asylum can be a little different, especially if you are a voluntary patient, because you can leave whenever you want. I needed to stay though, because had I left early in the treatment I knew I would be wrapped around a pipe within an hour of walking out of the door. I was determined.

I had never been an addict at any time and I wanted to beat this at all costs, so I remained where I was and did all that was required of me. I did all of the occupational therapy, including tying strings around tacks and making pretty pictures. I found a lot of it very amusing but at that moment in time it was far better than being in some motorway lay-by sucking on a can like some frenzied demon.

I completed my course and came out on some very heavy prescribed medication which I still take to this day.

I had been diagnosed with depression many years before and sertraline was to be my saviour, it seemed.

These antidepressants that I have to take regularly seem to hold me down and keep me balanced, and in times of crisis the medication is increased or lowered depending on my mood. I discharged myself in a very healthy state and set about getting a little direction in my life once again.

The best laid plans can soon go awry once you leave a controlled setting, and although I began to take drugs again, it would never involve a crack pipe. That has been maintained even to the present day, and although I look back on my early days of using it with fondness I am certainly overjoyed I beat that particular demon.

I still had many demons to contend with but I had left a very nasty one in my slipstream and it is now a fading memory. It would be difficult for me to re-enter the established routine I once had with my former associates, because they were not prepared to believe that I had cleaned up my act. They did not have the opportunity to witness the lengths I had gone to because a lot of them lived many miles away, and my world would not be sufficient to convince them otherwise.

I had begun to settle in Nuneaton now and was building bonds with my birth mother and extended family. My mother was still grieving due to the murder of her sister in a horrific manner. I will go into more detail on this matter in a later chapter that coincides with another incident.

But for now my funds were a little low, and for obvious reasons I am not prepared to name the department store involved, except to inform you it was a very major one.

Quite a few of my brothers and friends were playing cards in The Wellington public house and I was idling around by the bar, unable to afford the ante in the card game.

Two of the younger boys who we knew from the town came bursting through the door and whispered to me they had been play fighting against the doors, and as they fell against them they realised the doors were open; being as how this was a Sunday evening, nobody was in attendance.

I got two of the older boys to come down with me and investigate the situation further.

Once inside we had a quick look around to ensure nobody was around. It soon became apparent that we had the complete store to ourselves and a quick phone call was made to arrange transport. Meanwhile, we began to stack any amount of goods by the main door that we knew would have a ready market. Once again, I cannot detail the items or that would implicate me and others in the crime.

A small van was parked nearby and once we had been given the thumbs up that the nearby streets were deserted, we would rush out with our arms laden with as much as we could carry. This was repeated many times and on each occasion the van was full to capacity, it would go and be offloaded at my flat while we began the process of piling goods by the main door again.

All in all I would calculate we were in the store for the best part of five hours.

We decided to conclude business for the evening rather than run the risk of encountering patrolling police once it was closing time for the pubs in the town centre.

We went back to the flat and it took half of the night to detail item after item and get some sort of inventory of what we had. We were staggered to realise we had just short of forty thousand pounds' worth of goods, mostly by way of clothing – what a result.

We would need to be careful and none of the clothes would be able to circulate in and around Nuneaton.

I had always kept strong bonds with my criminal-minded friends in Yorkshire, and it was quickly arranged for our booty to be collected at the earliest opportunity and disposed of on the market stalls of Leeds. In all situations like this it is necessary to take a loss so that everyone involved can earn a little. Agreement was reached and we shook hands on fifteen thousand in cash and a kilo of amphetamine sulphate.

The amphetamine could be diluted to a lesser purity, thereby making the return a little larger, but we would not even need to do that until a later date.

For now, we were in the money.

We gave the young boys who relayed the original news of the store being open a little something for a drink themselves. We then proceeded to share out the rest equally between the three participants and a little earner for the driver.

Even the most reformed criminal would have difficulty in refusing a gilt-edged opportunity of that nature. Never look a gift horse in the mouth.

When we would sign on at the dole we would toss a coin for who went in to sign on first.

Should the police ever be searching for anyone, sometimes the first port of call would be to make arrests when a person came to sign on. It never happened.

No one was ever even questioned for the incident – happy days indeed.

High five to the person who made the mistake of leaving the door open.

You have my eternal gratitude.

CHAPTER 17

I had by now made the full move down to Nuneaton and decided to put the north behind me, except for the occasional drive up to watch Leeds United at the football or to do a little exchange concerning villainy.

The area being swamped with all of the football fans would make an ideal setting for doing anything untoward, which we did almost every time we visited the area. I would never miss an opportunity to visit my son while I was in the area, and unless we were doing anything that required being vigilant, he would be driven back down the motorway to spend a week with me and my ex-partner's father would come and pick him up the following week.

I would never lose contact with him right from the very first split with his mother. I have intentionally left my family situations out of this book, so I do not cause offence or intrude in their lives. Their private lives are exactly that and I feel duty bound to honour that.

I was fortunate on one visit when my son had been dropped to me at maybe eight years old. I entered a public house with him that we all usually frequented.

When I reached the room they were in with my full pint, they informed me they were just about to leave and go to the town centre, just for a few drinks, and they would be returning.

They all seemed in high spirits but luckily for me I declined the offer of a lift and instead decided to stay and play pool with my son. A long time passed and they had still not returned and I had given up hope of seeing them the rest of the day.

A customer came into the pub and expressed alarm about a crash that had taken place earlier, and I listened intently, realising this could involve my brothers and friends.

Fortunately the car was overloaded, and this is what perhaps saved some of them from serious harm. It transpired the driver was showing off, swerving the car from side to side in a street full of double parked cars either side of the road; once he lost control of the car and hit the first parked car, he would be thrown from one car to another in a pinball effect until the car finally rolled four or five times and came to a rest a little away from the crash scene that had resulted in eleven parked cars being extensively damaged.

I thanked the lord I had already bought a drink and declined getting in the car.

My brother said he had come around from a semi-conscious state and could immediately smell petrol at the scene as he kicked the glass out of the rear windscreen.

Everyone managed to escape the scene, albeit with the odd injury that needed treatment at the hospital, but it would not be possible because of the awkward questions and the police being notified because the car had been stolen earlier in Leicester.

Never a dull moment in and around our company, it seemed.

I squeezed my son tightly and breathed a sigh of relief.

I don't know what it was with me and cars but I had survived a bad crash only a few years before in Yorkshire and climbed from the scene, while others had broken limbs.

At least I had survived.

An incident involving a car full of young teenagers on our estate had not been so lucky, with the deaths of four of them.

My brother had recently taken over a pub at that time called The Donnithorne Arms.

The youngsters would gather at the pub and be served even though they were underage. Cheap alcohol smuggled from France at that time could be bought from anywhere around the estate and we, all of us in our youth, have managed to purchase alcohol.

These youngsters would have been no different, but they had also come and drank in "The Donni" and my brother was heartbroken later at the news of the deaths of these youngsters.

The barman had followed the usual pattern of spinning a luck fortune wheel and whichever drink the arrow landed on, that would be the drink sold for half price throughout the happy hour.

On this fateful evening the arrow landed on a particularly potent lager called Premier, which everyone consumed eagerly.

After they had left the pub, a very serious car crash took place resulting in the deaths of four of these kids and only the one survivor.

It was a tragedy our estate will never ever recover from as we are a close-knit community, and their places in our hearts and minds will forever be held dearly.

I have watched many of their siblings grow with time and the pain never lessens.

There was a little ill feeling at the time towards the pub, which was maybe a little uncalled for, but I could also understand the anger.

The self-same situation could have befallen my own family on the day the stolen car overturned, and if I am honest the crash concerning myself in Yorkshire could have also had a much more disastrous outcome.

All of us should heed the dangers of speeding around and I am thankful I survived my crash, but it would be too late for these youngsters.

God bless your souls.

There but for the grace of God go any one of us.

There would be an atmosphere towards the pub for a period of time until it was finally regarded as a tragic accident that could have taken place irrespective of alcohol consumed on the premises.

Things would return to normal but none of them will be ever forgotten – rest in peace.

Your memory lives on amongst all of us.

We had endured family tragedies of our own and not long before I had arrived in the area my mother's sister Margaret Barnes was murdered in the middle of the street after an altercation between her son and the son of the neighbour next door.

The case can be found on a site on the internet called "Fallen Angels".

A South African man called Dee Nayer cut my aunt's throat with a machete in front of her small children.

His defence was that he had suffered racial abuse and the judge indicated that this was the most significant aspect of the case.

Unbelievably, the man was given a two-year suspended sentence.

No amount of racial abuse, if indeed it took place, should account for that man's actions that day.

I wish you all to remember these events because of later incidents of tragedy within the same family.

My mother had a nervous breakdown at the time of this incident because she was very close to her sister, and I am not sure she ever fully recovered.

I still to this day witness the trauma that man

caused throughout the family, but one incident especially would cause me great alarm.

I was residing at some bedsits in the centre of Nuneaton when some young boy trying to impress me showed me some photographs and said, "You won't know about this but some blackie cut a woman's head off."

I grabbed him by the throat and told him in a threatening manner that this was my aunt, and how dare he have photographs such as this in his possession?

I was absolutely disgusted, but as I relaxed my hold and sat down he fled the scene.

On further investigation it turned out he was the stepson of a major detective in the Nuneaton police force who had taken quite a liking to my mum and her sister. But to keep things like that in his possession is quite perverse and unbalanced behaviour.

The name of this sick and twisted individual is Ollie Clarkson, who due to this and other matters, found himself suspended from the force.

My mother demanded to see the photos but I lied to her that I had burnt them with consideration to her previous breakdown.

I had in fact given the photographs to a Mr Chris Pendle from Rotherham & Co Solicitors. Chris was also a family friend and he would certainly know what path to take regarding them.

I kid you not.

These pictures were enough to repulse even the strongest of stomachs.

I could not believe what I was staring at and the memory will never leave me.

The body lay in the street with chalk marks around it and what I can only describe as a river of blood accompanying it.

Inside the man's house, he had placed the machete he used in the toilet pan and the toilet water and surrounding area were completely claret in colour.

These photographs will never leave my mind. I felt physically sick and could look no longer.

An outside force would be sent for to investigate these matters, and I would need to speak to two officers from Leamington who claimed to be the 100% genuine copper, who did not even believe in as much as a clip down the cells.

That remains to be seen, I thought to myself.

The conversation did not get off to a good start when I expressed concern over his colleagues still on the force, and any repercussions this may have on me.

Mr Clarkson by now had been suspended after the discovery of many stolen items in his home. These had been stolen from various police station property rooms.

I was asked how I knew that the photographs were not, in actual fact, newspaper clippings.

I replied, because I had been to crown court on instances of violence myself.

His response staggered me as he asked, "Why? Bit of a Jack the Lad, are you?"

I was furious as I asked him if that mattered at this

time, as the matter in hand involved a bad apple of their own. A sick and twisted individual who was meant to be a shining pillar of society.

After completion of our discussions I was assured that should I ever feel I was being needlessly harassed then do not hesitate to call them on a number they gave me on a card.

It is important to remember this part of the story for events that unfold in the coming months, but for now I had as much trust for this pair as I would for any member of the force. None of them were genuine.

Police investigating police don't cut it with me, I'm afraid.

God bless you, Aunty Mag, and I heard the bastard who did that died last year so I will drink long and hard to that.

May your soul rest forever.

We will all keep your memory alive.

Should any of you wish to know a little more, then visit the site mentioned previously and say a little prayer.

She did not deserve to die in that manner and I curse the bastard who did the deed.

CHAPTER 18

The twisted individual that was Mr Ollie Clarkson felt he had done little wrong and made a point of coming to live on our estate, and seemed to be constantly trying to wind us up and make us aggravate the situation by coming and drinking in our local "The Donni".

He would have no need for the half of lager he would order each day as he walked his dog. He would just be bold as brass as he stood amongst us, baiting us to hit him. None of us would ever physically assault him but he would always leave covered in saliva which we had flicked on him with our fingers.

He would brag openly that we had done him a favour because he had been given the chance to retire on medical grounds, and he would be receiving his full pension.

I wanted to smash this man's face in for his inconsideration towards our family, but I resisted the temptation to put him in a hospital bed.

Some of you may not like the next course of action that was taken but on his next visit to the pub and while he was busy taunting us, one of our younger brothers doubled back through the estate and broke into his house and spread faeces all over his furniture.

Justice is served a little and I don't care who is offended.

I would have loved to have been a fly on the wall when I imagined him returning to his home in a jovial manner, believing he had yet again wound us up, and was greeted by the scene.

Touché, you wanker!!!

Our main concern had always been his colleagues who remained on the force and I was most certainly being targeted, as I endured two early morning raids which resulted in discovering not one shred of evidence.

I knew I was being watched and I knew I was a target, so why would I need to do anything to put myself at risk?

I was aware an undercover operation was going on and cameras had been installed in the allotments over the canal and across from my flat.

The hardest thing for me not to do was to wave across to them, letting them know I was aware of their little games.

Once they realised I was not about to incriminate myself in any way, these two plain clothes drugs squad officers invented a complete cock and bull story as to what they had witnessed me do, and I laughed at them during the interview in the confident belief none of this could be proved or would even reach a courtroom.

This pair would be typical of any undercover duo the length and breadth of the country. A regular Starsky & Hutch pairing with torn jeans and designer trainers.

I doubted the evidence would stack up but to be on the safe side I contacted the two investigating officers from Leamington to express my concerns. Where was Cilla Black when you needed her? Surprise, surprise.

Nobody wanted nothing to do with me and I had been hung out to dry.

I did not even get the courtesy of a conversation.

This is the way of our police forces, ladies and gentlemen, and I very soon found myself standing in a dock at Warwick Crown Court accused of intent to supply drugs, although my fingerprints were not on any of the evidence provided.

I would not mind betting that a certain officer not in the force anymore could come into the equation.

Many of you may feel that this would not be possible but you need to trust me when I tell you that many police stations revolve around murky waters. You may disbelieve as much as you like but for now I had the added discomfort of trying to convince a middle-class jury at Warwick that the police are capable of fabricating evidence.

Oh dear.

A very unenviable task that did not reap any reward at all.

The sentence was three years' imprisonment because I had dared to question the evidence and I had incurred the cost of a three-day trial. Don't ever dare take on the system or you won't like the outcome.

I am bitter to this day about how I was fitted up, but to bring it into perspective a little, I laugh at the countless crimes I got away with to balance it out or the bitterness would eat away at me.

I would challenge any of those bastards at that trial to stand and look me in the eye and say they told the truth, the whole truth, and nothing but the truth.

I do not wish to alarm any of you but one of the officers concerned had reached the highest rank in Warwickshire the last time I recollect seeing his name up in lights.

A commendable man indeed.

My standards and morals are way above many of you people.

Yes, I readily admit I have been a bad little bastard at times, but what makes you any different? If you don't mind me asking. Bearing in mind you are all meant to be upholders of the law and upstanding pillars of the community.

I suffered a miscarriage of justice and my aunt certainly did, and more tragedy is set to befall my family in the coming chapters, with yet again an unfavourable outcome.

I am prepared to let the matter lie and condemn it

to history. All hail the sheriff, the new commander of the county.

I sleep soundly in my bed at night knowing you are in charge of proceedings.

The last I heard of the suspended officer, he had formed a partnership with the mother of a friend of mine which would have been awkward in itself, but things would get much worse.

My friend's mother was concerned about his behaviour and had tasked the lover to take charge of the situation and have a "fatherly" chat with my friend. The chat escalated to the man dousing my friend in inflammable fluid while he slept, with the intention of setting him alight.

The relationship with the mother soon broke down for obvious reasons as it became clear very soon that the man was in need of assessment for mental issues. I would have thought that would have been recognised much sooner than it actually was, to be honest, but who am I to find fault?

I would be expected to be anti-police, I suppose, but I am sure you will appreciate any animosity towards them is not without foundation.

The three-year sentence was quite a strange one because I ended up at a jail called Featherstone in Wolverhampton. This prison was full of some very rare characters who were in for some very gruesome crimes.

I had taken to reading an author called Dean Koontz and the librarian had noticed this and made a point of putting this author's books to one side for me after befriending me. I later discovered his sentence was for sleeping with corpses at the mortuary where he worked – Jesus Christ!!!

From then on I shuddered every time he spoke to me.

Another was for raping his own mother.

I was dumbfounded and took the decision to have little or nothing to do with all of them.

As always I had settled on educating myself and sat a Royal School of Arts degree in communication skills. The tutor had noticed I had no intention of assisting some of the others and pulled me to one side to inform me I would be failed if I didn't enter into the group education that was required.

I told her she could fail me if she wished to do so because I had no intention of assisting people who were inside for crimes which I deemed despicable. Rapists and paedophiles do not sit well with me, and I would rather cut their throats than ever even pass the time of day with them, let alone assist them in any shape or form.

I would be given special leeway because the female tutor had taken a liking to me and wished me to do well.

The sentence quickly passed and for a change I would have regular visits on this sentence from my partner of the time and my two small boys. I respect the privacy of my children and wish to keep them out of anything to do with my memoirs.

I am estranged from them and do not wish to complicate matters.

The sentence passed and I was about to hit the

street running.

It was the early nineties – the summer of love.

Ecstasy had arrived and I would soon become embroiled in the love drug and cuddle everyone I came into contact with.

CHAPTER 19

I needed to readjust and attempt to come to terms with the real world. That had been a long sentence for me to complete and I was in no hurry to return. I knew to live in this world I would need to turn my hand to anything that was available regardless of how poor the pay was.

Firstly, I planted saplings at the side of the motorway for the Forestry Commission for a paltry sum of £15 per week. Needless to say that job lasted a matter of days rather than weeks. I begged every employer imaginable to give me the chance to bring back some sort of respectability back to my life and household, and it eventually paid off and I was set on as an industrial cleaner at British Timkins, a bearings plant in Daventry.

It would be a half-hour drive away from Nuneaton

and I would be picked up by a works van at 5.00am every morning.

My big problem was that I had quickly settled into the party scene again, and especially the taking of ecstasy. I would get into the works van on a morning finding it impossible to make any eye contact with my other workmates due to my state of mind. Fortunately, we would never have any management on sight responsible for us until later on in the shift. We were contract workers and I would take the opportunity to go and catch up on my sleep in the warmth of the boiler room on many times.

Having a job was all well and good but the times that this employment coincided with were the headiest periods that this country would ever experience, and never to be repeated again.

Nevertheless, I managed to hold the job down for a good period of time.

Daventry was a smaller town in comparison to Nuneaton and I would have a ready clientele from this town wishing to sample this new drug, ecstasy. I would be able to charge as much higher price than what I was purchasing the tablets for myself, and some weeks the profits from the drug sales would even eclipse my wages from the actual employment.

It seemed I could never escape being involved in criminal activity no matter how hard I tried, and although I had only just been released from prison for similar offences, here I was, involved in the self-same practice.

I would always feel a little safer doing it from a controlled setting like a shop floor in a factory because it is much different to selling to random strangers in pubs and clubs.

The wages were poor and I had to improve them in some way.

Even my actual job gave me access to every area within the plant as my duties involved emptying the contents of each and every dustbin and replacing a clean bin bag, but while doing so I would come into contact with every single person employed there.

It soon became common knowledge that I was the man to see for just about anything.

I had other side-lines such as cheap perfumes and aftershaves that were in actual fact fakes, but I would assure people they were from ram raids. But the most lucrative trade would be the ecstasy. I was paying eight pounds each for and selling on for twenty pounds a time. Dennis the Menace, M255, Doves, China Whites, or any branded name of the time, I had access to them all and no shortage of customers as the club and rave scene had taken off in a very big way and these pills would be in great demand.

I would be nicknamed Doctor Death in a light-hearted manner, but I was one doctor the patients would rush to see before the weekend approached.

Occasionally some of us would take a pill at work if production levels seemed to be at a low, but it would never be something I would advise because a situation could soon go out of control and these sort and strength of pills would only be for the headstrong. Any chinks in your armour could prove disastrous and a workplace is far from an ideal setting for anyone likely to lose control.

I had learnt this lesson on a previous occasion when I had been asked to go up high on a mobile crane and change some lightbulbs that had blown. Even now, for as simple as the task seems on paper, I have never felt in as much of a dangerous place as I was that day. Even managing to drop one of the replacement bulbs from a great height and just miss one of the employees working below, and rather than offering an apology of sorts, simply laughed hysterically instead and for all to see.

When I wasn't working I was busy helping my brothers put on warehouse parties, which were proving to be quite lucrative.

Something had to give and it turned out I let the job go. It was interfering with my social life and I should have regretted that way of thinking, but looking back now I am more than happy I savoured that time.

Nothing before or since could even come close.

My best memories are during this era and outdoor gatherings with thousands in attendance would be commonplace.

Camps would be set up and makeshift stalls selling alcohol or food, and others brazenly selling drugs openly with blackboards chalked up detailing the "products" available and the prices. This was the closest to anarchy that this country had ever seen and I most certainly wanted to play a big part of it. In the blink of an eye large areas of land would be taken over by the masses and loud music would boom from every corner of the site.

Obviously the police would appear but by this

time the scene would have been set and they would just observe from a safe distance.

All of these gatherings began to cause great concern to all parties in central government, and in particular the Conservative Party who were in power at the time. Margaret Thatcher would rush through a bill called the Criminal Justice Act which basically denied us the right to gather in any great numbers listening to what they deemed "repetitive beats".

These sort of gatherings had shaken them to their roots. They were fearful of it gaining any more momentum than it already had. It wasn't as if they were losing any of their voters because none of us at these gatherings gave a flying fuck which party was in power, as we had no interest in politics and politicians had no interest in us.

I would have thought that a more appropriate law to pass at the time would have been a preventative one to stop any number of MPs gathering for paedophile activity and repetitive abuse of small children.

Thousands of us gathered in central London to protest the introduction of this bill, but all to no avail as it was rushed through Parliament at breakneck speed to prevent any more of what they deemed to be illegal raves.

The game was up.

It left the door wide open to big business entrepreneurs to take over and fill in the void left behind, and although some of the venues would spare no expense on lavish entertainment and laser shows, it would never quite be the same again. The loving, cuddling, caring attitude had gone, to be replaced by bouncers in suits recruited from the football terraces or regular night clubs.

God forbid that you ever tried to do any business at these events without their prior approval.

Things had turned very nasty overnight and the atmosphere had changed completely.

I had friends who would be pulled from the queues outside these events. They would then be taken to offices within and strip searched. If any amount of pills would be found they would be confiscated, along with any money, and they would also find themselves brutalised for even daring to consider competing for "in-house" profits.

These were not the sort of people to be messed with and this same scenario quickly spread to all other major events. Huge profits were to be made and the rave scene had quickly been taken over by these people, all working hand in hand with each other.

The days of hugging and having fun had long since gone.

It had been fun while it lasted but it was time to step aside and depart gracefully.

CHAPTER 20

This period became a very dark one, with many incidents of violence.

Prior to that did anyone really care if twenty thousand people gathered in some remote field for the purpose of an illegal rave? There would never be any trouble and security was never needed at any time. The government took it upon themselves to pass legislation and bring it all to an end, but wrongly so, in my view. At many venues people would remain after it had finished and clear all of the rubbish and a true community spirit could be witnessed on a large scale.

The people gathered would be described as anarchists or subversives but this was far from the truth. The media hype created a lot of ill feeling and prejudice but I can honestly say I never felt safer than in the company of these so-called undesirables.

I will give you an example of the so-called civilised members of our society, and judge for yourselves who needs castigating the most.

Bartley Gorman, a well-respected travelling man who was a good friend of ours, had a caravan situated in a few acres of land by Uttoxeter Racecourse. Bartley was the undisputed bareknuckle fighter amongst the gypsy community. He was a fearsome man but at the same time a very genial character who offered friendship to anyone and was the perfect gentleman.

Bartley had won many bareknuckle fights and could often be seen running through the local woods and keeping himself fit in preparation for any possible future fights. This man's strength was amazing and it would be a brave man who would dare stand toe to toe with him.

He would run amongst the trees and occasionally stop to punch one or two of the trees. I met Bartley on a few occasions and could not wish to meet a more polite gentle giant in his everyday life, but in a fight situation, he became a totally different person and totally focussed on what was required of him.

He was the undisputed king of his sport for many years.

Fortunately for Bartley, my nephew was staying with him in his caravan at the time the local community took the law into their own hands.

Bartley had been letting some of us put the odd rave on within his land and although the attendance would be reasonably small I would readily admit the noise would be rather excessive. Andrew Evans, my nephew, had lived with Bartley for quite a while at the time and it was a pleasant setting.

Some of the locals decided to approach Bartley and not only offer him an amount of money to move on elsewhere, but also land in Wales if I remember correctly. The offer was declined many times and I think Bartley enjoyed watching their discomfort with his rejection of the offers.

At some stage of the proceedings some of the group allegedly took matters into their own hands and one evening Bartley's caravan was set alight, with the assumption he was not in the area at the time. Unfortunately, Bartley was asleep in his caravan and had it not been for my nephew Andrew raising the alarm, the outcome could have very much led to a fatality.

Andrew performed heroics and dragged Bartley from the blazing caravan and the incident seemed to cause a great deal of media coverage due to the mysterious undertones surrounding the events of the fire. I praise my nephew often for his actions that night because had he not gone into the blazing caravan then I doubt that Bartley would have survived.

If the allegations are true, then shame on the people who would go to such extreme lengths to gain what they deem to be a satisfactory conclusion to their demands. I know for sure which sort of community I would prefer to live in and it certainly is not that one.

I have heard it said in mitigation that Bartley was believed to be out of the area when the incident took place, and therefore the intention was never to cause anyone any physical harm. It matters little to me and in no way condones such behaviour.

Shame on all of you who endorsed those actions and should it be true, I hope you have had many sleepless nights.

Middle-class suburbia and the creatures that lurk therein.

Actions that belong in the Middle Ages, to be honest.

I have never wished to visit Uttoxeter since this incident took place and I have even declined a day out to the races because it was in close proximity to Bartley's field, and I would much rather banish the memories of that day to history.

We would still attempt to put our own little parties on but by now it was all to no avail. Orders had been passed from above to all police forces that raves must come to an end at all costs.

We have always had close links to our local motorcycle gang, the Outlaws, and the Warwickshire chapter even have their own clubhouse in Nuneaton.

It comprises of two flats knocked into one with any number of tradesman within their club managing to do all of their alterations to the properties themselves. The exterior is strongly reinforced with steel shutters due to the long-standing rivalry with their sworn enemy, which is any Hell's Angel of the various chapters throughout the country. We would be invited to many of the events at the Outlaws' clubhouse and once inside, the safety of all inside is ensured.

I know many of these men personally and can assure you now that they are a sight friendlier than the media will have you believe. In actual fact they are very similar to my own close circle and in most instances are very beneficial to the local community.

Many of you may feel it is not the way forward for local gangs to be policing their own areas but that is the way of the world now. Not in a vigilante sense where instant justice is meted out. But I can assure you that should things go missing from our neighbourhood I would much rather ring around my close contacts to redeem those items, and it would be vice versa should the roles be reversed.

It can take days for most police forces to even respond to a crime, let alone bring it to a satisfactorily conclusion, whereas my own local contacts and knowledge are able to narrow the field down within hours and in most instances the goods will be returned.

I do not know how much safer you feel knowing this information, but I can assure you it is true. Blame it on what you will, government cuts, under-policing in whichever area, or even lethargy and disinterest on the part of the police. In the times we now live the majority of crime goes unreported and is dealt with internally by local people. Most of the people you believe you live in fear of are, in actual fact, your saviours.

People are too quick to prejudge others and it serves no purpose unless you know that individual on a personal level.

While in attendance at the Outlaws' club house I

would come across some of the most fearsome personalities you would ever care to meet, but many of these same people became long-standing friends and their loyalty is without question.

Yes, they may have been involved in many violent altercations with other rival gangs, but that is their own feud and does not implode onto the general public. They would not wish to harm anyone that did not wish harm on them.

I have had many amazing nights in and around these people and at least we had all found somewhere to continue our cosy little party period. On these occasions the police would choose to ignore our activities. We would be indoors and I suppose their policy would be that they knew exactly where we all were at any given time, so just turn a blind eye to it rather than antagonise the situation.

Had they ever taken it upon themselves to even attempt to enter the premises they would have quickly realised that any effort would be futile due to all of the very strongly reinforced doors.

For a change we would monitor them on the interior CCTV rather than them monitor our movements.

It was a very safe haven.

A sort of Nuneaton version of Eldorado and ensconced within were Ali Baba and his forty thieves.

The outlaws were a very organised outfit and had purchased a quarry in South Wales, and we took the joint decision of putting a rave on at this remote venue. The convoy that took off to Wales from Nuneaton was so big that it soon came to the attention of the police as we drove through various counties.

They were very intrigued as to our destination but that information wouldn't be forthcoming.

Eventually they must have taken the decision to scramble two of their helicopters and set up major road blocks. What was all this in aid of? The resources used that night were a disgrace and none of us had come this far to simply turn around and go home.

That was never going to happen.

Cars and vans were abandoned at the roadside and we made our way across fields, and our only source of light came from the full beam of the helicopters. Thank you for your assistance, officer. They had intended to herd us together but in actual fact guided our paths in.

What business was it of theirs if we were holding a party on land owned by the Outlaws?

No sir, we are here now and we were going nowhere.

They had confiscated one sound system on the way in but within minutes our other one was up and running and we had the pleasant sound of our "repetitive" beats again.

I think we stayed two days on that occasion and perhaps only really left because the drug supplies had run low.

The camaraderie at these events would be very special, especially when you realise that is was bikers and scooterists.

None of those silly rivalries surfaced during that period.

Ecstasy put paid to that.

That particular drug brought more people together who were sworn enemies than any other drug before or since. It became increasingly difficult to put any decent event together and many of us had to bite the bullet and accept that if we still wanted to party we would need to accept the introduction of the new licensed venues with all the trappings of fun fairs and exorbitant food prices, and everything geared toward emptying wallets.

The game as we knew it had gone. Who cared? By now we had become far too busy smuggling huge shipments of drugs from Holland.

It would cost us dearly as many of us switched from ecstasy to taking cocaine.

We never appreciated the violent times ahead.

It would be an eye-opener.

CHAPTER 21

With the introduction of these money-spinning clubs and outdoor events, all of the violence increased tenfold.

Coventry is close to Nuneaton in the Midlands and there has never been a lot of love between both areas at the best of times, but this period magnified the animosity.

One of the most famous clubs from the rave period was the Eclipse in Coventry and many a mad night would be spent in there swinging from the rafters. In attendance would be people from all corners of the country and from as far afield as Scotland. Everyone was expected to know the rules and none of us would have any clearance to sell tablets within the club.

All interior business transactions in that

department belonged to the security on the door or whoever they had nominated to be their runners. If any of us got caught in any way doing any trade, you would need to know the consequences. Caution would be needed, any slip-ups would result in a severe beating.

The in-house profits would be very lucrative and anyone daring to compete with these people needed to be a very brave individual indeed.

Early days, the club had a very ambient atmosphere, but it would soon change.

When you have been in a club all night on some very potent ecstasy tablets the last thing you would need on leaving that club at 6.00am would be a few of the locals wanting an early morning fight, but that's exactly what began to happen.

It would not be very difficult to single out who was a friend or foe.

Many club-goers would have a very uncomfortable night if we were "working".

It's difficult to say no because the profits are vast and not to be snubbed.

If any of us were unlucky enough to be marched up to the office, it was an experience that would set the knees knocking. These gentlemen never exchanged pleasantries. You would be stripped and then have any money or drugs confiscated and of course the usual dig in the ribs or on the jaw. It was mad days and par for the course.

On an uneventful evening it would be possible to leave the club with a thousand pounds, or in the worst scenario you could leave with no money and a fat lip and a drug debt to a dealer, because what you had done was had his drugs confiscated.

It's just a territorial thing, I would guess, but I have had more incidents in Coventry than any other area I can remember. Even years later when Oasis headlined at the Ricoh Arena, the situation was no different. One or two ambled into our company on the pretext of buying cocaine; in reality they probably had their own and simply wanted to observe if we were doing trade on their patch. After a slight interval one or two kicks were aimed in our direction until a big circle ensued and a full-on fight erupted.

Meanwhile Noel Gallagher, the founding member of the band, shouted over and over for order.

Was he for real?

Did he not get these confrontations in Manchester?

We held our own and an uneasy truce was called but for the odd punch here and there.

Minor skirmishes took place again outside the arena but it was no more than we expected when we began our journey over for the concert.

Any excursions to Coventry could be sure to have the hairs on the back of the neck going into overdrive. It would be no different from other areas, I suppose, and the need to have a great deal of awareness about oneself.

Over the years I have met and done business with a lot of the major players and now see some of them in a different light. The younger generations still fight with each other but us older ones have learned to put past difference behind us and earn money.

On the odd occasions when we could not get supplies we would be able to purchase in Coventry or vice versa.

On one particularly quiet period with a shortage of drugs in both areas, a friend of mine was sent to Manchester to buy £10,000 worth of ecstasy. This trip was not pre-arranged and the decision was taken at short notice to send my friend on a mission to find the amount we thought we would need to cover the hiatus until our regular supply was back in place.

My friend's name was Baron and many people in Nuneaton will know of who I speak, but for obvious reasons I need to protect his identity.

He was dispatched with the money with a warning to be cautious while up in Manchester.

At the time Manchester was one of the drug capitals with regard to purchasing ecstasy and we had no need to be concerned that a purchase would go ahead.

Baron unfortunately had stumbled across a couple of chancers who had decided to set him up in a sting to steal the money. He was told to wait on a street corner and have the money ready in preparation for the exchange.

They pulled their car alongside him and after holding up a bag seeming to be full of tablets, one of them held out his hand for the bag with the ten grand in. After a quick exchange, Baron was squirted with pepper gas all along his face and received minor burns to add to his embarrassment.

Before the two robbers departed they had thrown

their bag into Baron's lap, only for him to discover it was a bag of chocolate smarties. He was fearful of returning to Nuneaton and facing my brother, whose money he had lost, but luckily at that time we were involved in large-scale smuggling and money was no objective.

It was obvious by the burns on his face that the robbery had actually taken place and the incident was put down to experience, although Baron is still teased to this day about the time he was had in the net by a couple of streetwise Manchester boys.

Let's face facts, it's not a robbery which can be reported to the police. It's a bad twilight world out there which many would struggle to come to terms with. It can be a very dangerous place to make a living and it's not the sort of glamorous lifestyle you are all led to believe.

The rewards can be very great, but it's fraught with danger whilst you are earning those riches.

I could never complain at this time, on odd occasions I would be paying more for one night's accommodation in a hotel than I would have earned in a week's wage in a factory.

Times were good but it would be a very unnerving way to earn one's crust.

Firearms had now become more matter-of-fact which did not sit too comfortable with me.

A friend of mine, James Fenton, was ambushed and shot in the head as he sat in his car and to this day no one has been charged with the murder. I have watched his children grow and have every sympathy for what they have had to endure with the loss of their father.

James Fenton, or Irish Jim as he was more commonly known, may you rest in peace. God bless your soul.

Everybody had become very edgy indeed, and the drug of choice now, cocaine, did not help matters with increased paranoia. I had taken cocaine for many years but not to the extent it was being used now. The area was awash with the stuff. I would go days at a time without sleep and most days without food.

The Donni had become a drinker's dream, staying open all through the day and night. The flats where I live even to this day were perhaps 50 yards from the pub, but it would take me two days to come home for a change of clothes.

It was all very helter-skelter and one day would roll into another, as some poker games in the pub would go on for days, with piles of cash on the table and the occasional set of car keys.

Invoices would be ignored and as quick as one brewery took the decision to stop delivering barrels, then an order would be placed with another brewery.

This pub was as lawless as any you may see in the Wild West of America back in the day.

A prettier bunch than you could ever wish to meet used the place and there were no candidates here to enter into any beauty contest. Broken noses and zigzag scars could be seen on many of the faces. The pub had seen many temporary managers come and go, some of them making for the exit within a month.

A decision was reached, with the owner of the pub

to lease the place to one of my brothers but for obvious reasons his name could not be over the door as the licensee. No magistrate in this town could ever grant approval to any one of us bearing the surname Ginnelly, because there would be strong police objections and that policy is still the same to the present day.

I can understand this to a point but even so, it leaves a bad taste in the mouth knowing that future generations of our family are likely to be tarred with the same brush irrespective of whether they are upstanding and of good character.

It is a heavy burden to carry as I myself found out when I had first come to the area and found myself asked to leave many pubs simply because of my surname. Unjustified really, because I am of a very friendly nature and when I go out to socialise I do not even look for an argument, let alone a fight.

With the sort of pub, we had thought it went hand in glove that we would attract other undesirables similar to ourselves from other outlying areas.

On one such occasion an ex-boxer called Spider from the next town along, Bedworth, came into the pub brandishing a shotgun and threatened a few of the customers at the bar. This would be a very unnerving moment for many people but in our world at that time it was quite run-of-the-mill.

While one of the lads caught his attention and distracted him, one of my close friends just hit him hard on the jaw with his fist and knocked him clean out. Spider was then dragged outside, had the butt of his shotgun smashed into his face, and was left there in a heap.

My friend came back in and chalked his pool cue and resumed his game.

Spider was taken in an ambulance and had a police guard placed at his door for fear there may be further reprisals.

The damage had already been done really, and the police could never gain any convictions because evidence would always be in short supply with any incident that took place around us.

In Bedworth Spider has gone down in folklore in his home town and is regarded as a legend for having the nerve to come into our stronghold of a pub the way he did. I am not sure about that because the outcome resulted in him being in a hospital for the next three days and there isn't anything heroic about that.

I have no doubt though that he has been bought many a pint while asked to recount the story to yet another avid listener. It's certainly not the sort of action I would be tempted into, taking on someone else's territory.

I value my safety too much and would rather be drinking a beer than sucking on a grape in a hospital bed.

The Donni was noted for many a violent altercation, as I am sure Nuneaton police will bear testimony to.

I don't doubt many other areas are just as bad as our own and have similar pubs, but as much as the police seemed to turn a blind eye to much of our activities, that was soon to change with the discovery of a cache of firearms in the flat next door to where I was living.

This was to be the final nail in our coffin.

The days of "The Donni" were now very much numbered.

CHAPTER 22

I had recently split from my partner who I had, by now, had three children with. I do not wish to discuss these matters short of to say any parent who deprives the other parent of access to the children should feel a certain shame in their actions.

I have no wish to go into any detail but would like to take this opportunity to say I love all of my children dearly and it could never be claimed I was not a good parent.

Many people within this estate signed a petition for me to take to court confirming I was, in their opinion, a very good parent and I even had an endorsement from the local school's headmistress saying I had always been a good father and parent and had always made myself available regarding my children's schooling and education.

I rest my case.

I have no more to say on the matter.

I will pick up the tread of the story at a later stage to clarify what took place.

But for now, the smuggling that was taking place had reached epic proportions and the money going through our hands was never ending.

One of my brothers bought himself a property, paying cash in a six-figure sum.

With the amounts of money that were passing through us it obviously became quite clear that we had begun to receive a lot of attention, in particular from the West Midlands Serious Crime Squad, and these sort of units do not go away easily.

They were the proverbial dog with a bone.

We had come under their spotlight and were now the focus of their attention.

It would not be too long before they caught one or two of our friends in very "live" situations with photographic evidence at locations in Holland and again in the UK. They would have no means of escaping convictions and would be sentenced at a later date to ten years' imprisonment each for importing what the police calculated to be five million pounds worth of cannabis resin.

This would be a major result for the investigative officers and I would imagine their only disappointment would have been the fact they did not have a few more of us stood in the dock looking at similar sentences.

But we need not kid ourselves that we were in the clear.

Our cards had been marked and handcuffs with our names on lay in waiting. The hounds had been let loose and the chase was on.

These specialist police are known to be very diligent in the manner they go about their work and they do not have the additional distraction of solving other crimes. They have specific targets to aim at and sadly our faces were now the ones decorating some pin-up board.

Caution would be needed because I for one did not wish to be languishing in some prison cell for ten years or more.

With the arrest of our friends the chain of supply had been taken out of action anyway, and so this made our decision to be cautious a little easier to adhere to because for the time being we had no merchandise to trade with.

Operations and observations from any serious crime squad can be allowed to continue for years rather than months, and it's wise to realise that these people get the bit between their teeth, and if you are a target then get yourself out of the firing line as soon as possible.

I quickly took the decision to find gainful employment and hopefully vanish off the radar as far as these gentlemen were concerned.

I managed to find work through an agency first at a Tesco distribution warehouse in Hinckley close to Leicester.

Eventually I impressed that much while working for the agency that I was given a full-time contract working for the actual company.

It was at this time one of the most amazing coincidences of my whole life took place.

The manager who interviewed me for the job was rumoured to have had many jobs throughout his life and had even worked as a circus clown. Luckily enough, I heard about another of his jobs at a later stage when I had already worked for the company a reasonably long period of time.

Had I heard about his previous employment in the early stages of my contract I would have made for the door in my paranoid state. It turned out the man had even had a police career and even worked for a serious crime unit — I kid you not.

This information took my breath away and months down the way during a coffee break I said to the man jokingly, "You never told me you had been a policeman." He replied by saying that had he done so I may have sat and said, "No comment," at the interview. We both laughed and saw the funny side of things.

It is obvious by the numerous homemade tattoos on the backs of my hands that I had not led a sheltered life, and that man must have realised that and was prepared to give me that chance to redeem myself.

I take my hat off to that man for having belief in me and I like to think I never once let him down while I worked there. Jesus Christ though, I wanted to hide from the serious crime squad then I get given a job by one of their former colleagues — beat that for a coincidence.

I picked a shift that fitted in with my lifestyle.

I would start at 5.00pm and finish at 1.00am.

The shift would pay more because of the awkward hours and everyone would describe it as the graveyard shift, believing there is little to do at that time of the morning. Little did they know "The Donni" would just be coming alive at that time of the morning.

I had no reason to believe that we would still be monitored by the police and I could often be seen in my work clothes even during the day when I was not working. I was more than happy to place myself at arm's length from these people and give the impression I was no longer a part of the proceedings. In reality I was in fact enjoying having some sort of routine back in my life.

I would always do over and above what was asked of me on every shift that I ever did because I felt a need to justify their faith in actually giving me the job. I had always been a hard worker but I had just not been given the chance to get my foot through the door.

After I had finished one early morning shift I came back onto my landing to the flats only to discover I could barely move for the number of armed police that were present. It was of no great concern at the time because any incident in my block always seemed to command a large police presence.

After an initial enquiry as to what had taken place was met with a wall of silence, I simply mouthed the words "fuck off". I made my way into my home and slept soundly due to that evening's exertion from my shift at work.

Upon awaking, I was alarmed to discover the police had found an Uzi machine gun and two handguns, plus a large amount of ammunition.

The whole estate was on lockdown and the young couple who lived next door were both remanded into custody.

The male eventually admitted he was looking after the caches of weapons without his partner's knowledge but refused to name who they actually belonged to. His partner was released without charge but Dale Campbell was sentenced to four and a half years' imprisonment.

For a while I was like a rabbit caught in headlights because of the close proximity of the weapons to my own property. This was now all very much a different level and the police wasted no time in raiding The Donni, and after discovering another handgun in the safe the place would be shut down and no amount of objections would be able to save it.

It was razed to the ground at the earliest chance and has now been replaced by a number of flats for single mums and ran by wardens.

The heart of the community had been taken away and everyone was left without a meeting place. For many months after the discovery the estate would be swamped with a police presence that had never been known before. These were the times that people were living in fear of being robbed of large amounts of drugs or money. I doubt the guns would have ever been used but it seemed weapons were in every situation.

There was the added discomfort of being under surveillance from major police networks and the paranoia that exists with the belief that every stranger encountered is possibly an undercover police officer.

Thankfully I had "jumped ship" at the right time, and hopefully the spotlight would manage to avoid me.

I need not have worried too much because after an altercation with my ex-partner and breaching my terms of access to my children, I found myself in Winson Green prison for several weeks.

I was completely out of the picture and used the seven weeks to reassess my life a little, set myself a few objectives and redirect my life. I came out with all of the best intentions only to discover my children had been taken away and out of the area.

Even though I had a legal ruling from a judge that I was permitted access three weekends out of four, I could never get this enforced because the police would claim it was a civil matter and they could not get involved. I have never seen my children since. My little girl Demi was four years old and used to run and dive into her father's arms and squeeze my neck as any four-year-old would.

She is now twenty-one years old and I have not seen her since.

Every morning I wake it is like three of my ribs are missing and the pain of their loss is immeasurable. The thing that sticks in my throat is the police decision to not become involved and uphold the letter of the law.

A judge had ruled in my favour and in my opinion your task was to ensure the judge's ruling was carried out to the letter.

As much as I have become a very tolerant person, the older I have become I can assure you of this, I will go to my grave with a very anti-police frame of mind.

I will never have any respect for them, as all I have ever known from them is brutality, corruption, and fabrication of evidence.

I have every right to feel the way I do, I believe.

I respect my children's privacy and do not wish to go into any more detail on these matters.

I will always love you all until my dying breath.

Maybe you will read this book one day, hopefully.

CHAPTER 23

Winson Green had been an eye-opener. I hadn't been in a prison for a long while but if I ever needed a reminder that a bed was always available for me, then I would much sooner realise that while serving a seven-week sentence than anything a little lengthier.

Prisons had changed very much for the worse and many of the prisoners would be taking heroin as opposed to cannabis when I was locked up in my younger years. I definitely did not wish to see the inside of a prison again and luckily I have managed to remain a free man since that sentence. It would be embarrassing, watching them scurry about like sewer rats as they sought their next fix.

I am ashamed to admit that I took heroin twice prior to my internment, so luckily for me I was already aware of the implication of its use. I had not injected, I might add.

I had smoked it through a tube of tin foil and I am eternally grateful to this day that I had an adverse reaction to it, and because of the continual vomiting and ill feeling on both occasions, I reached the conclusion it was a drug that I did not like.

I have lost a few friends to this devil dust and would recommend anyone to give it a very wide berth.

I had other issues to deal with at that time, and not least the absence of my children.

It had left a big void in my life, an emptiness that could never be replaced. I sought solace in my usual crutches in life. Alcohol and drugs became very much a daily way of life and I could not be consoled by anyone.

By now my brother had another pub but I would soon find myself barred from there as my behaviour became very erratic. I would spend many lonely hours in my flat and I would smash the flat and its contents up as my black moods deepened.

I knew I needed professional help again but I did not wish to seem weak, and so just let the situation persist until I was at breaking point.

I had always been treated for my depression but this was something else eating me away until even the slightest positive thought I had left was engulfed by negativity. In this scenario the solution becomes clearer, or seems to; with each day the thought process remains the same and it becomes a regular thought process, and committing suicide becomes quite a reasonable and acceptable solution.

I was at breaking point and I would not wish to dwell on that day, but after a failed suicide attempt I found myself in a private room at the local psychiatric unit and under very heavy medication. I would cry a river most evenings when I was alone because I had come out of prison feeling healthier and more positive than I had done for a very long time, and the rug had been pulled from under my feet and I had absolutely nothing to focus on.

I would need many weeks of full-on counselling but I still did not feel strong enough to leave the unit or the sanctuary it offered me. It would be a while yet, but a decision was reached that I would see a counsellor on a weekly basis at a local addiction centre.

Once I came out I knew in my heart I would lapse immediately.

If the choice is to sit and dwell on matters alone in a flat or go out and socialise but run the risk of abusing drugs again, the latter option is preferable. How could it be beneficial to sit alone in the very same setting that had created the attempt at taking my life?

I quickly returned to the daily ritual of taking drugs again, and in particular cocaine.

I vaguely remember I had not been to see my counsellor for a while and took the step to pop my head around the door. I didn't expect the cordial greeting that awaited me by my mentor, who told me, "This isn't working, Dave. You've missed two appointments and come now on a day and time you shouldn't."

I tried to reason with him and told him that if people really came to see him at a date and a time that they should then they really aren't abusing drugs.

My life was chaotic and full of madness and mayhem.

Jesus Christ, I can't even remember your name, let alone when I am meant to see you.

They had exhausted all options with me by now and he suggested I had a little acupuncture while I waited until he found time to see me. After placing lots of needles around one of my ears he went to see his next patient and promised me he would return soon.

When he came back in the room in an excited state he asked how I felt, obviously assuming it may have turned me into a changed man. "What a complete waste of time," I told him.

Did he seriously think I would no longer want a pint lager or a line of cocaine?

Sweet Jesus, some of these people must be crazier than me, I thought to myself.

No counsellor ever seemed to want me for any great period of time and it would be no exaggeration to say I have had in the region of twenty or more different ones.

Granted, I am a complex character and I would try the patience of a saint, let alone any one of these psychologists.

I would be ushered to the door with a friendly goodbye gesture and I would laugh to myself, imagining the poor sods reaching for the whisky in the filing cabinet with a sigh of relief. The last thing I would ever wish to be is complicated but sadly the way my life has panned out will always see me being complex.

I have lots of mental issues which I come to terms with on a daily basis, and manage to control myself. I was never destined to be born with a silver spoon and a privileged background, and in some ways I am thankful for that.

Having all the trappings of wealth is all well and good but where is the struggle in that lifestyle? I would much rather be at the bottom of the pile where it is possible to learn much more about one's own persona.

My life has been full of drama from the moment I was born and abandoned; it is not a path I would recommend to everyone but I learned from an early age the wicked ways of the world and how to deal with situations.

Times have changed to such an extent that it is no longer possible to see any professional counsellor on a weekly basis. You would be lucky to see one every three months now. Any of us with mental issues have been hung out to dry now because of government funding cuts.

I could go and see my psychiatrist next week and not have a problem in the world and be given my next appointment for three months down the way, and yet within a matter of a week have a crisis with nobody available to see me.

It has all become a ludicrous situation because I have many days when I am at a very low ebb and have nobody to turn to. I have to be strong for the sake of my grandchildren who now visit regularly.

Depression is a silent illness and I have now accepted I will always suffer from it no matter what medication I am given to take.

I try to maintain some semblance of order in my life which can take shape by way of incessant cleaning or even writing can be very therapeutic, which I do quite often.

My way of trying to come to terms with this illness is to occupy myself at all times and not sit and reflect on things.

I have been diagnosed as a manic depressive also but I take little heed of expert opinions.

I know I will never actually beat the illness and so I have to adjust my life accordingly to deal with it.

None of the so-called experts seemed to find the solution at any time and even when I would think I was actually building an understandable rapport with one, I would discover on my next appointment I had a completely different one.

All in all, a futile experience and I would soon lose faith in all that the medical profession seemed to offer as I would need to go through the exact same process again with yet another figure scribbling away with his pen. I would often leave their company feeling disheartened and as though nothing positive had come from the meeting. I had accepted, by now, the need to stand on my own two feet and put distance between me and my so-called saviours.

I will always need prescribed medication and through the years I have been given Valium, Librium, Prozac, and finally the latest new kid on the block, sertraline.

At the present time I am content with the place that I am at and especially now my outburst of violence seems to be on the wane.

All things considered, I was doing quite well. I had in the space of eighteen months lost my partner, my children, and my family home.

I had recently buried my stepfather and carried my birth mother's coffin, and these were not minor mishaps, these were major tragedies and I needed a great deal of time to come to terms with all that had happened.

If you take all of this into account, I am sure you will appreciate that I had every right to be in a depressed state.

I will never come to terms with the suicide attempt and it troubles me greatly, but I try and rationalise it as best I can.

If anything, I will never reach those depths of despair again.

I feel I am a much stronger person for my actions that day.

Onwards and upwards.

CHAPTER 24

I had hit rock bottom and I was the only one who could change the situation, but as always I set about doing it the wrong way.

I would have regular parties at my flat and this would be for two or three nights in succession. Random strangers would also show up alongside my many friends, and the music would continue all night.

Occasionally one of the neighbours would send for the police and they would show up in numbers with consideration to the recent discovery of the firearms. Matters would soon get out of hand with bottles being thrown at the officers and people urinating over the landing and down onto them.

Arrests would be made sometimes and an agreement would be reached to turn down the noise. Once the police had left the volume would be increased yet again. It amazes me even to this day how I managed to hold on to my tenancy. I would get letters from the council on a weekly basis asking me to come down and discuss the loud and antisocial behaviour.

I would always ignore these requests as I would be far too busy organising that coming weekend's party. Eventually common sense prevailed and I stopped all the madness and mayhem.

It had reached the stage where none of my neighbours would speak to me and I would resort to hanging my washing out late at night when I would be able to avoid contact with them.

I got myself into a bit of a routine and normality would soon be resumed. The only thing I lacked was some sort of work to occupy me that could give me a little focus.

Through an agency I got myself a position at a Lynx distribution warehouse that delivered parcels throughout the country.

Not before the stigma of my name had preceded me, though. The personnel manager rang the agency to see if they could vouch for me personally.

I was given a start but it soon became clear that many of the workforce had took a disliking to me and I would be allocated all of the difficult and heavy trailers to empty. I would try and maintain some sort of discipline but it reached the stage where I was carrying a small cosh into work with me and I had no doubt if this bullying persisted then someone was likely to get hurt – and it wasn't going to be me.

This shouldn't have been taking place on a shop

floor but unfortunately it was, and I would much sooner have dealt with it my way than make a complaint to the management. I would rather it had not reached this stage but I had no option. I had a bad habit of not turning up for my shift on a Friday evening and that could be explained quite easily by the fact that we got paid on each Friday and I would have been showing up for the shift having had a few beers.

Alcohol and a cosh in my inside my pocket made for a bad combination and I would much rather have not attended than cause injury to those people. Eventually an atmosphere must have been sensed and it was suggested to me a day shift may be available if I wanted to change shifts.

I jumped at the chance and only later realised I would be the best part of sixty pounds a week worse off. On the day shift it turned out my take-home pay would be two hundred and twelve pounds per week – I kid you not.

When you consider that twenty-five years previously I had been earning one hundred pounds per week more than that, it tells you what little progress the employment situation had made.

If you also take into account that wages in the north of England were meant to be much lower with regard to the cost of living, you will realise why I found the wage structure absolutely disgusting and leaving a lot to be desired.

I was now earning one hundred pounds a week less than what I had earned twenty-five years previously. But there had been no strength in Trade Unions, no more since the Tories had locked horns with the bigger unions of the steelworkers and miners. They had beaten them into submission but beat them they had, and with the defeats many workers' rights went out of the window.

We were all on a wing and a prayer and were expected to bite the bullet and doff our caps to the bosses who ripped us off each week. My only consolation to this was the Lynx warehouse was like an Aladdin's cave to a magpie such as myself.

I resisted the temptation for many months but in the end I got really frustrated at all the continual searches of myself and my locker. It was obvious that management had convinced themselves that any items going missing and stolen must be in some way connected to me.

I took this as an affront and took umbrage until I finally thought, *If this is the expectation then I will do exactly that.*

In the early days of this decision I concentrated on helping some of the poorer families on the estate with the odd few computer games. Do the manufacturers of these games understand the hardship that many working-class families go through, with the continual release of new games on a weekly basis with prices ranging from forty pounds upwards?

Any of the games I stole I would sell to these poorer families for ten pounds per game. The excitement and smiles on these small children's faces was priceless when I pulled the recent releases from my coat.

It would be more than worth the risk of losing my job. It seemed it was expected of me by management so I would gladly grant their wish. I had worked there for a while by now and I quickly recognised which boxes coming along the rollers were worthy of attention, and I would take full advantage.

Contracts for Game or Blockbusters would come through on a daily basis, along with JJB Sports or boxes full of new phones headed for the O2 shops.

Petty pilfering soon became richer pickings and the joke became that rather than employ additional security, why not weigh Ginnelly when he gets here and weigh him when he leaves?

If a new England football shirt came out I would once again take quite a few, and especially the smaller sized ones for the poorer children on the estate.

Initially I would only do it on the odd occasion but that soon increased to having something to supplement my wages on a daily basis, especially once I realised that almost everyone in the factory was doing the exact same thing. These other workers had been taking things all during the time the finger was being pointed at me, and they had found it funny that I had acted as a red herring for their activities.

The wages were poor and I despised the Managing Director because on the one occasion we dared to take some sort of industrial action, he simply drafted agency workers in from as far afield as Watford.

He also brought in what I can only describe as night club bouncers from Birmingham to break the strike.

If any of us on the picket line made any effort to approach the minibuses bringing in the "scab" labour, we would soon find ourselves being threatened by these individuals and could clearly see they had knuckle dusters on their hands.

It would not be wise to antagonise these men but a few of us swore that once we finally returned to our jobs we would make sure that we stole a sight more than we had done previously. The battle lines had been drawn. Was this the modern way of dealing with a strike, to be threatened with violence?

Upon returning I wasted no time in dropping a box of phones so heavily that the contents spilled out. A case of an item "falling off the back of a lorry" only in this instance the lorry was parked up in a warehouse.

Many of the phones were very expensive and in the five hundred pounds bracket, and a friend advised me that it was not worthwhile taking these phones because they would be locked and therefore could not be sold on.

But I have recently spoken to a friend of mine who had a contact in Portugal, and it turned out that once the phones were on a different mast in another country, then the phones would work perfectly. These phones could now be sold at half price and the phones would be the equivalent of a week's wage. And once again, stressed my contacts in the criminal world.

It seemed for me it would never be possible to completely break away from my criminal past, no matter how hard I tried.

If I ever thought that by being on the shop floor it would help me lessen my drug-taking lifestyle, I would be sadly mistaken also. Many of the young lads I worked with would bring cocaine into work and we would be consuming any amount of it in the back of one of the trailers.

Now and again we would hear the familiar chink of bottle against bottle from the inside of a box. We would tear open a corner of the box until the contents could be accessed and then partake in the odd bottle of wine until at the end of the same shifts we would be very tipsy from the alcohol and wired from the cocaine.

It was certainly some company to work for and especially the company I worked among.

You all know who you are – great bunch of lads.

We may have lost the industrial action but we gained a bigger victory in the end. Don't ever feel ashamed at what we did.

We deserved better recognition than what we got and what we did was justified.

Many of the children on the estate were probably in tears when the games dried up with the purchase and relocation of the company. They were bought out by American company, UPS, and each one of us was again given the chance to retain our terms and conditions of employment and move with the company to an alternative warehouse, perhaps some four miles away.

This would prove difficult for me as I did not drive, so I settled for the easy option and took the voluntary redundancy that was on offer. This was not a decision I took lightly because I had to consider my age and appreciate that I may not ever work again.

My health had been suffering for a while anyway

and I had been booked into Walsgrave Hospital in Coventry for some major keyhole surgery, so my decision was made for me.

I miss all of my workmates because this term of employment was very enjoyable and reaped quite a good profit. Should any member of management be reading this then take a bow, because you were correct in your assumption that I was on the take. That was the corner you all pushed me into if I am honest – no handshakes – no sad goodbyes.

I accepted the redundancy cheque willingly and departed the scene of the crash. UPS had taken the decision to employ their own management staff for the new premises and the staff at our branch were surplus.

How did you all like that, gentlemen?

You mattered little or nothing to them after all of your endeavours. I cared little.

I had my money in the bank and I had already spotted a hole in the market where I was going to boost my money.

I was about to begin growing cannabis. Nuneaton Council would not be too happy about my decision, I suppose. But cannabis cultivation it was to be, and this was my next career move.

CHAPTER 25

I had a very difficult period after the completion of my keyhole surgery, and it soon registered that I would be incapable of working again. I am also the same as many of you and have very demanding grandchildren who I had previously taken on holidays to Butlin's, and I would still need to do so.

It soon became clear that my redundancy pay would quickly run out if I did not find a solution to invest some of the money in, and although I was a little apprehensive at first I finally took the plunge and bought all of the equipment I needed to set up a little cannabis factory in one of the rooms of my flat.

I had never been a particular fan of smoking cannabis because on the few occasions I had taken it I would have great difficulty fastening even my shoelace, let alone functioning in a normal manner.

I would discover that the occasional joint would ease the pain and discomfort from my chest area since the operation and anything at this time that would assist me in sleeping through the night was a godsend.

Yes, of course I was breaking the law again but no more than I had been doing my whole life through, and from it being a sort of hobby one minute and providing alternative medication, it soon became quite a lucrative side-line.

I became very adept at what I was doing and my yield each time I cropped the produce was more than enough for my own needs, and I would have enough left over to make a very heathy profit.

I will explain later in the chapter what brought my activities to the attention of the police and the proverbial knock at the door, but for the best part of five years I would have no problems at all and more than enough money to meet my grandchildren's needs.

There is no room for any margin of error if the cost of purchasing all of the essential equipment is in excess of eight hundred pounds, and I took to my newfound task like I had done it my whole life, and soon got my first returns on my investment.

Through my contacts in the criminal fraternity I would never have a shortage of buyers, and because of the high grade quality of my produce I would usually have sold my wares within two days.

Only in very trusted circles would I give close friends a certain amount and give them "bail", which in effect means a week's grace to settle the bill. I would let them have it at a cheaper price, thereby giving them the chance to also earn themselves a little pocket money.

There were many homes doing the very same at this time and I imagine the police got a little irate about just how widespread it had become.

To be quite truthful, I didn't have any objections as to how I earned my crust. My overheads were quite steep on my first attempt and just in case my efforts didn't bear fruition and I took a loss, I decided to cut a few of my expenses with a shoplifting excursion.

Not just any shoplifting, I might add. I had noticed a lapse in security at the local supermarket where it was possible to come out the very way that one had entered the store.

I would go down aisle after aisle, filling a trolley with everything possible, and then amble back the way that I had come until I reached the electrical section of the store, giving the impression I was looking at purchasing a television set.

While in this section I would pull out from under my arm some carrier bags with the store's name on and spread them over the products in the trolley. This then gave the impression I had paid for my shopping earlier and I had gone to then look at purchasing other items to be paid for in that section. I would wheel my way out whistling towards the exit without a care in the world.

More often than not I would have two hundred pounds' worth of food and I would do it on a regular basis, until it must have come to the store's attention that this was far too much to be overlooked and extra store detectives were employed.

I could not shake this man off on one visit, and although I had a reason to be going down the aisles in reverse, he most certainly did not.

Just in case I was being paranoid I carried on with my usual procedure, albeit once I left the store I made a point of leaving the trolley in the doorway. The man, out of breath, rushed up alongside me but realised immediately there was little he could do because I had not left the store with the trolley so no offence had been committed.

He loitered about in the area, possibly thinking his chance may still come, but to make matters worse for him one of the store's female assistants returning from her lunch break greeted him by his Christian name and my heart sank for him (not).

If I recall correctly, she called him Brian.

After a polite silence I lit up yet another cigarette. I went over to him and put my arm around him in a consoling manner and told him, "I'm going to have to get off, Brian. I'm running a tight schedule."

He was taken aback by me confronting him, but it was obvious I would not be doing this supermarket sweep any more. Did it really matter? I probably had enough food to last for the next three months. Which was convenient because the cannabis grows in twelve-week cycles.

I imagined Brian cursed his luck that day and I also realised I had gone to the well to quench my thirst far too often, and had I kept my visits to a minimum I could have shopped at the same store for many years to come.

I still go in the same store now many years down

the way, but the loophole has long since been closed. It was a good little earner while it lasted. Slightly better than buy one get one free.

The cannabis would be growing at a very healthy pace.

I would need to leave many of the other electrical outlets off in the flat because the lights feeding the plants would consume a great deal of energy. I had been given the option of bypassing the electric but I deemed this to be a dangerous practice and could lead to my instant eviction from the flat should I get caught due to endangering my flat along with the other residents in the block.

I would pay for my electricity and would need to keep the consumption down in other areas so as not to cause any great concern and bring suspicion on myself. I wasn't exactly becoming a millionaire overnight. We are talking perhaps three and four thousand pounds each time the process was complete, but the money would be put to good use. In reality it was more per annum than I had been earning at my previous two places of work.

This is the way of the world I live in and what I would like you all to very much appreciate is that there are far more corrupt people in what is deemed the real world than could ever exist in mine.

I was harming no one and I will never apologise to anyone for my actions. In all walks of life, it is necessary to be durable to be able to survive, and that's exactly what I was doing.

The heart of western society is rotten to the core and come Judgement Day I doubt very much I will be at the head of the queue to explain my sins. Anyone who knows me will confirm I am an open-handed generous person who sees to others before myself.

I had progressed to being a cannabis farmer and I had no qualms whatsoever about becoming one. It was another notch on my belt, another addition to my CV.

Did anyone really think I was concerned by breaking the law? I had done that from drawing my very first breath, almost.

By now my sister's daughter had come to stay with me and she had asked me to keep an eye on the relationship she had with her boyfriend, because she feared he was hitting her. I was at a friend's party when I noticed him kick her very forcefully on the ankle, but I chose to ignore it out of respect to the household we were in.

After we came back to my flat I put some fat into a pan under the pretext of making some lunch.

When the fat looked reasonably warm I shouted the boyfriend into the kitchen and asked if he would like a coffee.

As he neared me I used the element of surprise to smash the coffee cup into his forehead and as he sprinted to open the door of the flat I threw the fat in his direction. He bolted down the stairwell and never resurfaced until a few days later when I gave him a very firm warning that should he lay one finger on my seventeen-year-old niece again, I would stab him in his buttock and show no mercy.

He assured me he had understood the message loud and clear and he would correct his behaviour.

All seemed well until I saw my sister in town and she was inconsolable regarding a beating her daughter had recently taken.

The more I investigated, I discovered the boyfriend had carried my niece from my back bedroom with his hand over her mouth so he did not disturb me while I slept on the settee. He then took her down the canal tow path close to my flats and gave her a severe beating, but being careful with regard to facial injuries.

I find this sort of behaviour totally unacceptable, and had I not already warned him what his fate was likely to be?

I arranged for my niece to be babysitting at another address where she wasn't even needed.

I warned all of my close neighbours to not come out should they hear any noise at a certain time, and then they would not witness anything. The trap was set and I waited for my prey.

When he finished his day's work he came up the stairwell with his usual arrogant attitude, asking where my niece was. I confirmed that she was not there but I was, and in one sudden lunge I stuck the knife into one of his buttocks and watched him scream in agony. I pulled him to the floor and I would have possibly caused him a great deal of harm but for the fact one of the older residents ventured out to peg a few clothes out.

My victim ran along the landing and stood by the old lady, believing he had found sanctuary. He then proceeded to run to the phone box and send for an ambulance.

Obviously with it being a physical injury the police were obliged to put in an appearance but by now I had long since vacated the area, burnt my clothes, and disposed of the knife.

This retribution may seem very harsh but the only concern I had was in respect of the old lady who I went and found at the earliest opportunity once the police had conducted their door-to-door enquiries.

Let me first explain, I look after all of the older residents in the flats and check on them regularly and do any shopping they need. When I knocked on Maureen's door she ushered me in immediately and gave me a very big squeeze, saying she had been concerned for me.

I apologised sincerely for what she may have witnessed that night and told her she must know that was not the real me.

She shocked me by saying that she had heard my niece's screams the night she was beaten because she lives close to the canal, and that I should do whatever I pleased to the "bullying bastard". She informed me that she had swilled the blood away from outside of her flat and told the police that she had seen nothing, God bless that lady.

Nothing ever came of the matter because I knew he would never dare recount what had taken place in any court of law.

I kept his injury to a minimum even though his wound needed stitching, and I would hope that every time he sees his scar it will act as a sharp reminder to not brutalise women.

I would have got away with this incident but my

name would be in the headlines and they would soon be back knocking at my door.

Nuneaton Police don't ever go away.

CHAPTER 26

Within a few months I had taken my little Jack Russell, Stella, for a long walk, and when I came off the canal I could see the all too familiar yellow van that the police had been using on the estate to carry out early morning drug raids.

Once I came onto the landing of the flats I could clearly see that my door was being knocked. I attempted to retreat down the stairwell but it was too late because I had already been seen, as one of the officers shouted, "Oi, Mr Ginnelly! Could we have a word?"

There was no way out of it and I would need to invite them in. I was asked if I had anything in the flat they should know about before they conducted an extensive search. I simply remained silent but realised the impossibility of being able to conceal a very large

Buddha tent and all of the accessories that were with it.

Once the officers came back downstairs one of them said, "Unfortunately you are under arrest for cultivation of cannabis." He then indicated that another gentleman wished to speak to me, which he did, and said in a very stern voice he represented Nuneaton & Bedworth Council and my tenancy was now terminated.

I doubted that very much but he insisted that I either give him my keys there and then voluntarily or he was going to pursue the matter down legal channels.

I thought to myself, *Well that's the route we are going, Mr White Collar Worker.* In my view it was a trivial manner; it wasn't like I had a body in a vat of acid or something equally sinister.

They were all overreacting a little bit too much, and no way would I be walking away from my home of my own volition. I was put in handcuffs and taken down to the local police station along with the residents from two of the other flats, all of us under arrest for the very same offence. "My, my, you have been busy," I joked to one of the others.

He could not understand why I was being so flippant but many of my friends had recently been arrested for the self-same thing and it had simply resulted in a caution. A sort of reprimand, a slap on the wrist, call it what you will but I know the likelihood was that I wouldn't even need to go to a courtroom, let alone face a custodial sentence.

I would be held in a cell for the next seven hours while interviews were conducted.

Even though it had been a while since I had a taped interview, it all soon came back to me, how to conduct myself. It's very much a game of chess.

In my earlier days it was possible to remain silent and say, "No comment," time after time, but that ruling no longer exists. The process becomes one of very cagey questions and answers with the intention of the interrogator to try and implicate others in the offences.

This would never be possible with me because I have never implicated even one person in my life. That sort of treachery would never sit well with me and I despise any person that does it. It would be tantamount to selling my soul.

The interview went on for perhaps an hour until it became clear to the officer that nothing else was forthcoming and it would be wise to terminate the interview now.

Of course there would be knowing winks and smiles across the table but as always, I am very careful what I say orally while a tape is recording. I was placed back in a cell and informed that because I had not been very helpful that I may now be here for much longer than was first anticipated.

He had played his ace card and perhaps he thought it may get a positive response. "Don't worry," I told him, "as I will have a little sleep while I wait."

A matter of a few additional hours meant nothing to me.

Once I was finally released I was informed that I was being given a caution with regards to my future behaviour, but I would not be facing any charges –

surprise, surprise.

I was told not to forget that I would need to go immediately to see my housing officer regarding my tenancy, but I would disregard that request. I had just been in the cells for seven hours and lost my source of income.

I would not be wishing to sit in yet another long, drawn out conversation.

It was the nearest pub for me while I drowned my sorrows.

When I got back home all of my tent remained in the bedroom, albeit being in a very slashed up state of disrepair. The police policy, it seems now, is to take away the actual plants but leave everything else behind for the owner to dispose of. Obviously they do not leave anything which may make it functional again.

I could not bring myself to even go in that bedroom for the next month or so.

I was very dejected because I knew it would not be possible to set up the process again, even though I had the funds available to do so. I had also been given a year's probation by the council to correct my behaviour, thereby retaining my tenancy.

I would not wish to jeopardise my home and so I needed to search further afield to source an income. The police seemed to be paying me a lot of attention, although it may have been other residents in the flats.

Each time I left my home they seemed to be parked up out the back of the flats.

I had spoken to a few of my friends in Yorkshire and they had come across a married couple who ran a highbrow estate agency, and they were responsible for the sale or letting of many millionaire properties.

I was asked if I would like to be involved in a very big cannabis factory they were intending to set up.

The married couple had been involved in one previously but the Vietnamese people who they had trusted had run off with the yield as soon as it was ready to cultivate.

A friend and I took the decision to go up to Yorkshire and see if it would be possible to set this up on a large scale. The property chosen was a very large manor home surrounded by similar properties. The married couple would simply take this property off the market for a while, thereby giving us ample time as we needed.

This house had its own gym, cinema, and snooker room, accompanied by stables and both an indoor and outdoor swimming pool.

This was the life, the lap of luxury.

We soon settled into our lush surroundings and would have food delivered by some of our friends under cover of darkness at regular intervals.

For obvious reasons it would be wise for none of us to be spotted in the area.

We looked what we were – a very unsavoury-looking bunch who could scare a vampire back into his coffin. The decision was taken to remove the seating from the cinema and after an experienced electrician bypassed the electric, we were ready to put the equipment in we would need.

Cultivation on a scale such as this would most

certainly lead to a lengthy prison sentence so caution would be needed. We would take it in turns of two of us babysitting the produce in a week on and a week off shift.

We would look quite a comical bunch because at no time would any of us take our surgical gloves off for fear of leaving fingerprints if anything should go wrong at short notice and we needed to flee the property.

Our toothbrushes and other items would always be kept on us as we did not wish to leave any DNA evidence within the property. It may all seem a little extreme but the profit margin involved with a production and cultivation on this scale would be immense.

The intention was to do it on a few occasions and hopefully the seven of us involved would have enough money to retire on for a while.

The plan would be to return everything back to normal in the cinema once our task was complete, but things would never go according to plan and someone would make a healthy profit out of this enterprise, but it certainly wouldn't be me.

I doubt very much that it was a case of loose lips sink ships.

I was thankful it wasn't my turn on shift but on reflection, maybe if I had been, the finger of suspicion would have been pointed at me less.

When my friend and I were in attendance at the property we would help ourselves to alcoholic drinks from out of the cabinet and have many games of snooker. The curtains and blinds would always be closed at the property, giving the appearance of being unoccupied for safety reasons.

It was an ideal setting and very remote, but this setting would also make it easy for what was about to happen next.

If indeed it did.

Apparently the two friends of mine who were in charge of the duties for that week heard some noises and went out to investigate, only to be confronted by four men in balaclavas and two of them armed with handguns.

In situations like this it is futile to steal the produce if it hasn't reached its final stages because the strength of it would be second rate and very inferior, and therefore unable to be sold. But this was perfect timing.

They had hit the jackpot and after apparently terrorising my two friends they took away everything that had matured in the two hundred pots of soil.

Everyone blamed everyone else and set about pointing the finger.

The suggestion was that the assailants had Birmingham accents and so the blame was pointed in my direction because I lived close to Birmingham. I suspected the married couple because I was loath to suspect my friends, who I had known for many years. I was angry that the suggestion was that it was to do with me, because I had strong links to the Midlands.

Because of this suggestion I now began to suspect the two who alleged they had been robbed had chosen to deflect suspicions in my direction.

It's a situation nobody would welcome because it

is impossible to involve the police or get Columbo to search for clues.

It's a no-win situation.

Long-standing friendships have ceased to exist because everyone blames everybody else, and there are so many possible different outcomes that it is impossible to reach a satisfactory conclusion. Someone got greedy and decided to have the lion's share of what we produced, but it certainly wasn't me.

What I prefer to believe is that if the married couple lost a lot of money when the Vietnamese had stolen from them, they had taken the second lot simply to compensate for their previous loss. If that was the case and there really was four sent to the house that night, I'd like to think that they then stole it from the couple. It would be rough justice indeed.

I had visions of living the high life for a while and all of my dreams had been taken away by whoever was responsible. I would never put any names up for inspection by the general public or the police while writing this book, but I have taken this chance to confirm to you that I know nothing of what took place that night. One or more of you do, though.

I feel betrayed by people who I regarded as friends and in actual fact, since that night I have never taken part in any criminal activity.

I was expecting to have a little retirement pot of money but instead I have decided to have the enforced retirement that the night brought about. Loyalties no longer seem to exist in the criminal world and it's all about who can make the most profit and it doesn't seem to matter at whose cost.

It's a sad situation to be involved in, but if anything it made me finally change my life around for the better. Who wants to be involved in any of these activities when it has reached the stage where it is no longer possible to trust even your close allies?

If any one of you involved still think that I was involved in any way, then you really need to look again at all of your conclusions.

I thank you for one thing while I have the opportunity.

It changed my whole outlook on life and the path I had chosen, and I conformed overnight to become the much better person I am today.

I was no longer a criminal.

It had been a long time coming but I had finally set about cleaning up my act.

CHAPTER 27

While I had been busy with the ill-fated cannabis factory in Yorkshire I had been neglecting my flat a little, and got myself positive and focused on getting it presentable once again in anticipation of having my grandchildren to stay on regular occasions.

The first job would be to finally dispose of the remnants of the tent that Nuneaton Police had left in my spare bedroom. I was becoming very depressed again because of the financial side of things but used the decorating of the children's room to restore positivity.

I disposed of the tent and anything that was to remind me of my criminal activities. I would change a room first, but then set about changing my life. I had always thought of my surname to be quite an unusual one, but with the introduction of the internet I soon discovered that many Ginnellys existed throughout the country, and even realised there were a few David Ginnellys.

Who were these imposters?

I have a very large family within Nuneaton.

My mother gave birth to six boys and four girls and one or two of them were making headlines for all of the right reasons, so what was preventing me from doing the same?

My brother Jimmy Ginnelly is a very well-known character in non-league football, who is presently managing a small village club in Barwell, close to Leicester. He recently made history by taking his small club into the first round proper of the FA Cup – by all accounts an amazing feat.

My sister's son Joshua recently signed a professional football contract with Burnley, and is expected to be a premiership footballer within the next few years.

This was the sort of fame I craved, but I seemed to have made a total mess of my whole life.

I had spent eleven years in various remand homes, detention centre, borstals, youth custody, and adult prisons.

I had been treated in two mental asylums and I hadn't planned on my life being so chaotic. It had just happened.

Don't get me wrong, I had seen more throughout my life and hadn't learnt much. I was happy that I hadn't lived a boring, mundane existence, but I had now reached the stage where I wished to live a little differently. Half of the battle had been won already because I hadn't been in a prison for many years and I planned on that continuing.

I had reached the stage where I no longer felt I had a need to prove nothing to nobody.

I command a lot of respect in my town but much of it was for the wrong reasons – I would set about changing that.

In my own block of flats, a heroin addict had recently been allocated a flat and he would need monitoring, but in next to no time he had many of his friends visiting, and some of the single mothers with children began to express concern.

I took it upon myself to resolve the issue and forced my way into the flat.

There was no furniture but the living room was littered with used needles, and once I went up the stairs a few of the residents could be found sat on a mattress around an electrical fire for warmth.

What I witnessed next still staggers me to this day.

A small baby in nappies squeezed my inviting finger I had put out and I glared at the mother as if to say, "How dare you have your baby in these surroundings?"

I made it clear they all had a few hours to gather their belongings and vacate the flat or I would unleash hell on them.

Needless to say, they left at the earliest opportunity.

I have always made every effort to look after all of the residents, and in particular the older ones. They always say they have a certain amount of comfort in the knowledge that I am close by, should I be needed.

The next unwelcome resident to come to the flats was one of the seediest individuals I have ever come across. Some of the residents had been informed he was a paedophile and they were rightly concerned. I said that I wouldn't become involved unless they had categorical proof that he was what they claimed. I told them to contact the local police station and as concerned parents, demand to be notified of the details to do with the person.

The confirmation sickened me.

They were told that yes, he had just been released from prison in relation to serious sexual offences against children, but their hands were tied because the tenancy was in the female's name and all they could do was suggest we remain vigilant and alert – really.

I went straight down and kicked the tin of paint over, and told them not to even consider decorating because they wouldn't be moving in. The woman expressed outrage that I had just walked into her home but by now I knew the full facts.

The paedophile had actually sexually assaulted both of her small daughters and one now lived with her mother and one with her sister. Christ's sake, where do these sort of mothers come from?

She had waited for him to come out of prison to rekindle her relationship. I find that disgusting.

No way were they going to be allowed to remain in these flats.

The police were sent for because the woman claimed I had forced my way into her home. I obviously denied this and after the neighbours on the upper landing confirmed that I hadn't even left the landing and had been with them for the past hour, the police knew they were fighting a losing battle and decided to leave.

I looked down at the paedophile and waved a claw hammer in his direction, and they quickly decided it would be unwise to actually move in.

Again, that may seem a little extreme but would any of you reading this care to have a miscreant such as that living in close proximity to any of your children?

They are natural predators.

I have been in many prisons with them and find them to be very repulsive people.

It was bad enough being housed in a prison alongside them, so if anyone thought I was going to live alongside them in my own neighbourhood then you are sadly mistaken. A lot of single mothers with small children lived in the flats at that time and my consideration, first and foremost, was for them.

Round about this time our local school was burgled and all of the funds for outings the following year were stolen along with the safe. Some of the children were special needs children and it saddened me that anyone could stoop so low.

It was believed that the burglars had got away with perhaps eight hundred pounds, so I set about fundraising to get the children the money back. I had come across one of the youngsters at the shop in tears at what had happened. I promised him faithfully that if he smiled I would recover the stolen money for him.

After getting the local paper involved and setting up a fundraising page, amazingly, within a week eleven hundred pounds was raised within the estate and the headmistress was overwhelmed with the kindness and generosity of the people involved.

It's these sort of people who contributed who make the world go around.

Money came from many local businessmen and from as far afield as Australia.

I may have been the figurehead of it all but could have done little or nothing without every last one of you.

In my first book, *Wellies and Warders*, I recount all of my spells of homelessness and living on the streets in Yorkshire and also in London. For this reason, I decided to become involved in the local charity, Doorway, which is responsible for homeless youngsters between the ages of sixteen to twenty-five. When I was asked to become involved I didn't even hesitate. Nobody understood the rigours of living on the streets better than me.

I had slept in a dirty old mail bag at the back of Euston Train Station in London when I was fifteen years of age.

I had every sympathy with what these young children were going through.

The people who run the charity, and in particular a lady called Carol Barnsley, have a very good aura about them, and even though they were all more than aware of my colourful past they welcomed me into the fold with open arms.

For my own part it gave me a little direction and encouraged me to be that positive person. I would still have the odd incident in my life as I will explain in a later chapter, but I was enjoying the newfound me and especially once I realised all of the influence I seemed to have on people.

I could contribute very little because I was now seemingly destined to be on benefits for the rest of my days, but I knew influential people who had the means at their disposal to make life a little more comfortable for those youngsters, and I would prompt them to become actively involved.

I had walked past the Doorway charity on regular occasions when I had walked to the town centre, and never once even realised it was a charitable organisation. I would always assume it was an estate agent as the name Doorway seemed to suggest it was to do with housing.

It's the reason I dedicated this book to those children and young adults, because it is now my adopted charity which I intend to become involved in on a regular basis. I am there most mornings and witness these youngsters come in from the streets in need of food and perhaps a shower, or access to the computers to check on the availability of employment.

Government legislation has now made it impossible for them to be provided with housing benefit, thus making them homeless, and due to them having no address the possibility of obtaining employment becomes impossible.

The misery they must feel about their situation can be seen etched on their faces on a daily basis. This country is meant to be one of the most civilised and rich in the western world, but I fail to see that, I'm afraid.

I have collected amongst my friends a good deal of monetary contributions, but have also got some of the local camping shops to donate tents, sleeping bags, hats, scarves, and gloves.

The people who run this charity are under constant pressure for funding and barely survive, but are genuinely dedicated people who will always find time to assist the poor unfortunate waifs and strays.

They are our responsibility as a community and are more than worthy of the assistance they receive.

The ones I have spoken to and offered a little advice, are the products of fucked up parents, and they didn't ask to be placed in this situation; their stories of sleeping under bridges and the like practically break my heart as I reflect back on my childhood shortcomings.

I had done many bad things during my life and here was my chance to absolve myself a little, and at the same time assist others less fortunate.

People started to regularly stop me in the street and place money in my hand, knowing full well that every last penny would reach its destination at the charity. It's a nice feeling to have, knowing that people trusted me implicitly and wished me well in all that I was doing to raise awareness.

I would raise issues with the local paper and bring matters to the general public's attention, and reach a very much wider audience. A mass sleep out on the streets in Nuneaton is planned also, at the time I am writing this book.

I suppose in a way I am also trying to redeem myself a little.

For these people to accept me the way that they have, gives me the feel good factor I have been lacking.

I still take regular medication for my depression and I suppose I always will need to do so, but occasionally when I feel myself begin to get a little down I think of the youngsters' situations to remind me there is always someone in a much worse position than myself and it can raise me a little.

I feel I have found my niche now in life, and will always be available to assist these young people in whatever way I feel I can.

I've been there and cried myself to sleep in shop doorways as a small child with little or no comfort from any of the elements should they choose to take a turn for the worse.

My heart goes out to these youngsters.

It's a fading memory now, with me, but I can remember being very afraid on certain nights out there.

It's a disgusting reflection on our society that this is occurring in our present-day society.

Some of them have no parents to call as such but have no fear, because I will attempt to be the father figure you require and the voice to speak in your defence.

Good luck, each and every one of you.

Please believe me, it won't always be like this.

Have faith.

CHAPTER 28

Which brings us back to the very beginning and the age-old question, "What makes a criminal?"

It isn't preordained and is never set in stone.

Circumstances dictate what we become but we all know right from wrong and each one of us has the choice as to whether we wish to stray from that path or not.

Although I regard myself as a very much reformed person, I would never safely say that should a situation arise where I could amass a great deal of money through some criminal activity that I would not be seriously tempted, because that would be untrue.

I will never be able to escape my past and I accepted that a very long time ago.

I have experienced some very scary situations and

although I firmly believe that I never made many enemies, I still never feel totally comfortable unless I have a few strategically placed weapons around my home – would any of you wish to live in this manner?

I doubt it very much, but to a person such as myself it becomes second nature.

I have weapons close to my front door and close at hand in the living room, and also at the side of my bed. It becomes a way of life and although many of you would find that strange it is completely acceptable and very much normal to me, and others like me.

I have many scars around my face as testimony to the many beatings I have taken. One side of my head has been numb and without feeling for the past twenty years from when I was knocked out with a spanner.

I have had my teeth smashed in by some person wielding a snooker ball while I was in borstal. I ended up in hospital for a few weeks on that occasion. My eye sockets and mouth area have a lot of scar tissue. I had my ribs broken by brutal and sadistic prison warders.

Is it any wonder I turned out to have my very own violent tendencies all during my formative years and beyond?

Only recently, prior to the writing of this book, I had a very violent altercation that could quite easily have resulted in me going back to prison.

I do get quite angry at the best of times and I had recently been referred by my psychiatrist to attend an anger management course. I found the course more amusing than anything else, if I am to be honest, on the occasions when we had to stand and confront the class to give our accounts of a very mild-natured incident.

I would be very uncomfortable with some of the things we would be asked to do and would often refuse. I was told I would be thrown off the course if I did not lay on the floor in a star shape holding hands with the others whilst listening to piped music of dolphins and whales screeching.

Was this for real? Was this really happening to me?

I suggested jokingly that while everyone was laid on the floor then why not place needles in our ears and we can maybe get some sort of double benefit. No, I'm afraid these sort of situations don't sit with me and have no therapeutic value whatsoever.

I made my excuses that I felt unwell and left the building.

There was no way I could have laid on the floor and become involved in what I deemed to be a farce.

I don't doubt that it may prove helpful to others, it just wasn't for me.

About this time one of my sisters had been working at our local pub and while mopping the floor one morning some "gentleman" had kicked the doors, demanding they be opened, and gave my sister some very frightening abuse.

She had told him the pub would not be open until 1.00pm but this was not the news he wanted to hear. Fearful for her safety, she vacated the pub and went into the nearby post office.

I knew nothing of this until a week or so later when this same "gentleman" came into the pub one

Sunday afternoon. He was again in a troublesome mood and began to push some of the customers around by the bar area.

I was asked to have a quiet word with him and put my arm around him in a friendly manner and asked what his problem was.

He said in a demanding manner, "You know what my fucking problem is, I want stuff." He ran his finger along his nose while he said this, obviously indicating he was looking to purchase cocaine.

I informed him that there was no stuff and it was time to leave, but still tried to maintain some sort of calm.

At this time one of my nieces began to shout, "Dave, Dave that's the man who threatened to shoot my mum!"

I was livid. I was never aware fully of what happened with this individual at the time that it had happened. This was now on a completely different level and I ran him out of the door and spun him round in a big circle.

By the time he came back around to face me my clenched fist was already on its way to greet him, and I made contact that took him clean off his feet. He was out cold by the time he hit the floor.

My problem was that I had made contact with his teeth and caused my knuckles a great deal of damage. The area around my knuckles had a great tear and was bleeding heavily, and I knew I would have to attend the hospital, but right now my main concern was that this person seemed lifeless.

People would keep coming in the pub saying, "He is still out, Dave." I had visions of facing a manslaughter charge.

He must have had a couple of friends who had been waiting in a car while he came and purchased his "stuff" and they had come to and dragged him along the pavement to their car.

I left it as long as I could before I went to the hospital as I was wary that the police would also be there due to the man's injuries.

By the time I went up the injuries on my hand had become so bad that I was transferred over to the University Hospital in Coventry for emergency plastic surgery. I have now lost the feeling in all of my index finger and the knuckle protrudes at an awkward angle.

I would be heavily bandaged and would need to have my arm raised in a sling for a week or so until the hospital were satisfied that I would heal sufficiently from the operation.

I decided that it would serve no purpose to show up at another anger management course the following day because I wouldn't be the best advertisement for the benefits of the course.

Incidentally, the "gentleman" was never seen again and I guess he realised that he had overstepped the mark and took his punishment on the chin – literally.

I do not wish to be that person anymore, who is renowned for unpredictable violence, but given the same set of circumstances I am sure many of you would do the same as I did. It was my young sister who had been threatened.

The area where I live can be a very unsavoury one at times and when my small grandchildren come to stay, at times the last thing I want them to witness is heroin dealers doing their trade outside of my window and along the canal.

Sadly, as in many other areas the police never seem to act on these matters even after considerable complaints, so what are the residents meant to do? I took matters into my own hands and confronted them and informed them that should I catch them by my flat, I would hit them with the hammer I was holding and then throw them in the canal.

Our problem is, gangs come to the area from Birmingham and Coventry and do their business by way of postal code areas, but I had made myself clear that CV11 was now off the agenda.

I prefer not to be that sort of person but sadly at times I am left with no alternative. At times it seems impossible to put my past behind me and just blend in to some sense of normality.

I accept that I command a lot of respect in the area but I would now rather that respect was channelled into more positive areas. Just walking into town with the grandchildren can take ages as everyone wishes to stop and talk with me.

I have to confess I do like the attention because finally in my life I am recognised and acknowledged for all of the right reasons. I have not been in a courtroom, let alone a prison for the past eighteen years, so I must be doing something right.

I do not profess to be a saint, but I have reached the stage where I will not risk my freedom again.

It has been a long time coming but I feel I am finally on the right path.

I would expect you all to appreciate that this is now the second time I've put pen to paper and wrote a book, but each time I do it I open up certain wounds and release skeletons I had long since buried.

I have lost many friends at a much younger age than what I am now. Drug casualties, murder victims, have led to them having much shorter lives but their memory will live on in my heart and discussions.

I was recently invited to be the guest speaker at the local Women's Institute and to say I was a little apprehensive would be an understatement, but I need not have worried. Those ladies made me feel comfortable in every sense of the word and I quickly found a sense of confidence that I did not realise I had.

The realisation that I could address a room full of people without seemingly causing offence confirmed to me that writing and talking was indeed my forte. I had stories to tell and an audience that wished to hear them, and I welcomed the warm applause and ovation I received at the end.

I later discovered I had been voted their speaker of the year.

I had always been encouraged to write by many tutors within the penal establishment but would never heed the advice given. It is possible in any prison to get access to the best education imaginable and I acquired many degrees while I was inside.

I had been asked by one of my tutors to consider entering some material for a Koestler award. These awards are given for creativity amongst inmates involving art, literature, or other subjects.

Koestler recognised that many talented people dwelt within our prisons and openly encouraged prisoners to demonstrate their skills. I had made a start on the project but on one occasion while I was being transferred from one prison to another, one of the arrogant officers (who are never hard to find) on duty asked as to what I had been writing about, then proceeded to describe it as "a load of bollocks" in his own words.

I had perhaps got ten chapters written but the officer decided that for security purposes I was not allowed to carry written literature from prison to prison, and that was the end of that particular vision.

No award would be coming in my direction but I am quite sure that had he put his mind to it the warden could have won a nomination – "Prick of the Year".

These are the sort of people you encounter on a regular basis and they are to be found in any prison.

It would be a while before I entered into anything again.

It would be pointless to complain to any of the tutorial staff because if they register a complaint all that happens is it brings trouble to your cell door. The tutor would have left the building and gone home but the warder would still be on duty, and with his big bunch of keys, could access all areas. I'm sure you get the picture.

But I wish I had taken their advice much earlier because my first book released went straight to the top of the Amazon bestselling chart for true crime within forty-eight hours of its release – I was staggered.

I could not believe what I had achieved, or the critical reviews I was getting.

I was a writer and thousands of people wanted to read my words.

I get stopped by complete strangers in the street who want me to sign my name in their book.

Wellies & Warders has changed my life for the better.

The response to the book has totally taken my breath away and I have taken the decision to continue writing due to the constant requests from people wishing to read more of my adventures in life.

This latest book is in dedication to many of my friends who did not manage to complete the journey with me, and in particular my twin brother who died in childbirth. What fun we could have had together causing double the trouble for the infamous DS Hurst.

I would have loved the chance for the both of us to give that man a constant headache.

God bless you, my never-to-be-met sibling.

Who knows, had you survived I may have turned out differently – on second thoughts though, I doubt it.

I have carried enough personality during my life for the two of us.

We will meet, but for the time being your presence will remain with me.

I hope to turn my life around now and I thank every last one of you for your continued support.

Enjoy the book.

All Saints school burglary

Godiva Festival with Whity & Ski

NEVER A DULL MOMENT

Isle of Wight Festival

Me & Gaz Kent

NEVER A DULL MOMENT

Me & Raff

DAVE GINNELLY

Me & Ski

NEVER A DULL MOMENT

Me in my tripping days

Paddy & Glenn, my brothers

Day out in Brum

Homeless Sleepout Doorway

NEVER A DULL MOMENT

Kev Hanson

Me & Lee Cass

NEVER A DULL MOMENT

Me & Ski, Godiva Festival

DAVE GINNELLY

Me & Whity

NEVER A DULL MOMENT

Me, Kadi & Stella

DAVE GINNELLY

TV interview